T0277751

VEGAN ONE-PAN

VEGAN ONE-PAN

70 EASY & SATISFYING VEGAN RECIPES
FOR EVERY DAY

rps

RYLAND PETERS & SMALL
LONDON • NEW YORK

Senior Designer Toni Kay
Senior Editor Abi Waters
Editorial Director Julia Charles
Head of Production Patricia Harrington
Production Manager Gordana Simakovic
Creative Director Leslie Harrington

Indexer Vanessa Bird

First published in 2023 by
Ryland Peters & Small
20–21 Jockey's Fields
London WC1R 4BW
and
341 E 116th St
New York NY 10029
www.rylandpeters.com

10 9 8 7 6 5 4 3 2 1

Text copyright © Ghillie Basan,
Liz Franklin, Tonia George, Dunja Gulin,
Kathy Kordalis, Jenny Linford, Hannah
Miles, Louise Pickford, Leah Vanderveldt,
Laura Washburn Hutton and Ryland
Peters & Small 2023 (see also
page 160 for full credits)
Design and photographs copyright
© Ryland Peters & Small 2023

ISBN: 978-1-78879-560-9

A CIP record for this
book is available from
the British Library.

US Library of Congress cataloging-in-
publication data has been applied for.

Printed and bound in China

NOTES
• Both American (Imperial plus US cups)
and British (Metric) measurements and
ingredients are included in these recipes
for your convenience; however, it is
important to work with one set of
measurements and not alternate
between the two within a recipe.
• All spoon measurements are level
unless otherwise specified.
• When a recipe calls for the zest of citrus
fruit, buy unwaxed fruit and wash well
before using. If you can only find treated
fruit, scrub well in warm soapy water
before using.
• Ovens should be preheated to the
specified temperatures. We recommend
using an oven thermometer. If using a
fan-assisted oven, adjust temperatures
according to the manufacturer's
instructions.

FSC
www.fsc.org

MIX
Paper | Supporting
responsible forestry
FSC® C008047

CONTENTS

INTRODUCTION

Plant-based diets have never been more popular. Once considered a simple support act to a meat or fish dish, the vegetable is now the rising star. The great thing is that we now have access to a superabundance of wonderful, versatile and healthy vegetables and fresh herbs, and increasing numbers of us are growing our own at home. We can easily shop for amazing spices and ingredients from around the world, and there are so many good things to provide the protein element of our meal without having to cook meat or fish, making a vegan diet easy to achieve. Pairing that with cooking everything in one pot or pan, will make for a much simpler and easier time in the kitchen. One-pan cooking not only saves on time but also on clearing up. Cutting down on the amount of dish washing and clearing away after preparing a meal, frees up precious time in today's hectic world.

ONE-PAN COOKING

This is just a brief selection of the different pots and pans you might need to create the meals in this book that will transform your cooking experience from laborious to speedy and efficient.

Saucepans with lids: incredibly versatile and perfect for making one-pot soups and stovetop casseroles or stews.

Casserole dishes/Dutch ovens/tagines: these are heavy-duty dishes with tight-fitting lids that are generally used for slow oven bakes and stews/casseroles.

Frying pans/skillets: investing in an ovenproof heavy-duty pan will give you much more versatility in the kitchen as you can start a meal on the hob/stovetop and then transfer to the oven to finish cooking.

Wok: generally used for quickly cooked meals such as stir-fries.

Roasting pans/dishes and sheet pans: buying good, solid pans and looking after them will serve you well and save money in the long run. Buy a couple of different sized pans to suit various meals and with a mix of deep and shallow sides.

A WELL-STOCKED STORECUPBOARD

The benefits of keeping a well-stocked storecupboard should never be underestimated – with quality always taking precedence over quantity. The best kind of storecupboard should be one that naturally calls to be restocked regularly as it's built on items you love to use almost every day. That way, you'll find that you can always rustle up something for supper if you've had an especially busy day.

BREAKFASTS

CHOCOLATE & COCONUT GRANOLA

- 190 g/2 cups rolled/old-fashioned oats
- 80 g/1 cup flaked/slivered almonds (substitute sunflower or pumpkin seeds/pepitas for a nut-free version)
- 4 tablespoons cacao powder
- 2 tablespoons chia seeds
- 1/2 teaspoon sea salt
- 1 tablespoon maca powder (optional)
- 60 ml/1/4 cup melted coconut oil
- 60 ml/1/4 cup pure maple syrup
- 45 g/1 cup coconut flakes

MAKES ABOUT 500 G/
3 1/2 CUPS

If you love your breakfast on the sweet and crunchy side, making your own granola is one of the easiest and most satisfying things to master. This version made with cacao powder tastes like grown-up chocolate puffed rice cereal.

Preheat the oven to 140°C fan/160°C/325°F/Gas 3.

In a large mixing bowl, combine the oats, almonds, cacao powder, chia seeds, salt and maca (if using). Mix together to distribute the cacao evenly.

In a pourable glass measuring jug/cup, combine the oil and maple syrup, and whisk together with a fork. Pour the wet ingredients into the dry and mix together until the oats are evenly coated.

Spread out in an even layer on the prepared baking sheet and bake in the preheated oven for 20 minutes. Take out the sheet, rotate it 180 degrees, sprinkle the coconut flakes on top and bake for another 15–20 minutes.

Note: If you smell burning at any point, take out the baking sheet to cool a little, stir the mixture and turn the oven down slightly. Return to the oven for the remainder of the cooking time or a little less. Remove from the oven and leave to cool completely on the baking sheet – this is when it will really crisp up and get its crunch. Once cooled, break into pieces and store in an airtight jar at room temperature for up to 2 weeks, or in the refrigerator for up to 1 month.

CLASSIC MIXED OATMEAL PORRIDGE

- 70 g/½ cup coarse oatmeal/ steel-cut oats
- 50 g/½ cup rolled/ old-fashioned oats
- 2 teaspoons apple cider vinegar
- 500 ml/2 cups water, plus more for soaking
- 250 ml/1 cup dairy-free milk of your choice
- ¾ teaspoon salt

OPTIONAL TOPPINGS
- berry compote
- toasted coconut (see right)
- sliced fresh fruit (such as banana, strawberries or kiwi)
- chopped dried fruit (such as cranberries, pineapple or papaya)
- add-ons for texture (such as pistachios, chia seeds, freeze-dried raspberries or blueberry powder)
- brown sugar or pure maple syrup

SERVES 2–3

This genius yet simple combination of coarse oatmeal/steel-cut oats and rolled/old-fashioned oats gives a creamy, yet textured consistency that is super satisfying.

The night before, combine both types of oatmeal/oats with enough water to cover them by about 5 cm/2 inches and the apple cider vinegar. Leave to sit at room temperature for at least 8 hours.

The next morning, drain the oats and rinse them. Transfer to a medium saucepan and add the water, milk and salt.

Bring to the boil, then reduce to a simmer. Cover with the lid slightly ajar and cook for 10–15 minutes, stirring occasionally. You want most of the liquid to be absorbed but the mixture should be loose and not gluey. If it's a little too thick for your liking, add more water and milk and stir in, cooking for a couple of minutes more.

Serve with your desired toppings.

TOASTED COCONUT

- **45 g/1 cup large unsweetened dried coconut flakes**

MAKES 45 G/1 CUP

Preheat the oven to 160°C fan/180°C/ 350°F/Gas 4. Spread the coconut flakes out on a baking sheet lined with baking parchment. Bake for 3–5 minutes until golden. Watch the flakes closely, as they can burn very quickly. Leave to cool. Store in an airtight jar or container at room temperature for up to 2 weeks.

SLOW-BAKED PECAN & COCOA NIB GRANOLA
WITH GOJI & GOLDEN BERRIES

- 250 g/2½ cups jumbo oats
- 100 g/¾ cup mixed seeds (sunflower, hemp, sesame, linseed, chia, etc.)
- 50 g/1¾ oz. solid coconut oil (or substitute olive oil)
- 50 ml/3½ tablespoons brown rice syrup
- a pinch of salt
- 150 g/scant 1½ cups pecans, roughly chopped
- 100 g/3½ oz. golden berries
- 100 g/3½ oz. goji berries
- 50 g/1¾ oz. cocoa nibs

MAKES 10 SERVINGS

Long, slow-baking gives granola a lovely flavour and crunchy texture, making this an absolute winner (and much cheaper than store-bought). The texture will be a little more free-flowing than non-vegan versions, but in no way lacking in flavour. Serve it with a good dollop of your favourite coconut yogurt and some fresh fruit, adding a drizzle of date syrup if you fancy a little extra sweetness.

Preheat the oven to 130°C fan/150°C/300°F/Gas 2.

Put the oats and seeds into a bowl and grate in the coconut oil (or add the olive oil). Add the brown rice syrup and salt. Stir until evenly mixed. Spread over a roasting pan and bake for about 40 minutes, until the granola is golden and crisp.

Add the pecans and return to the oven for a further 5–10 minutes, until the nuts are lightly toasted. Remove from the oven and leave to cool before stirring in the berries and cocoa nibs. Store in an airtight container at room temperature for up to 2 weeks.

ROAST RHUBARB, BLACKBERRY & BLUEBERRY COMPOTE WITH COCONUT YOGURT

- 400 g/14 oz. rhubarb
- 200 g/1½ cups blackberries
- 200 g/1½ cups blueberries
- 60 g/5 tablespoons caster/granulated sugar
- 60 ml/¼ cup boiling water
- seeds from 2 vanilla pods/beans
- 50 ml/3½ tablespoons Grenadine (optional)
- 400 g/scant 2 cups coconut yogurt, to serve

SERVES 4

This three-fruit combo tastes every bit as lovely as it looks. Oven-roasting is a perfect way to cook rhubarb – it keeps its shape nicely (so long as you don't overcook it and scoop a little too hard to get it out of the pan). A generous trickle of Grenadine is an optional extra, but it will add the prettiest pink blush to the juices – it's a lovely ruby red syrup made out of pomegranate seeds (although do look out for the Real McCoy, as the cheaper, almost fluorescent brands are often just a mixture of corn syrup and colouring).

Preheat the oven to 170°C fan/190°C/375°F/Gas 5.

Trim the rhubarb and remove any stringy bits. Cut the stalks into 3-cm/1¼-inch lengths and arrange on a large, deep baking sheet. Scatter over the blackberries and blueberries. Mix the sugar and boiling water together in a jug and add the seeds from the vanilla pods. Stir in the Grenadine (if using) and pour the mixture over the fruit in the pan. Cover with foil and roast for about 12–15 minutes, until the rhubarb is just soft. Remove from the oven and serve warm, with the coconut yogurt.

BAKED OAT MILK PORRIDGE
WITH PEARS, ALMONDS & DATE SYRUP

- 160 g/1¾ cups jumbo oats
- 1.2 litres/5 cups oat milk
- 75 g/½ cup mixed seeds
- 2 teaspoons vanilla bean paste
- 1 teaspoon ground cinnamon
- 3 medium ripe, but firm pears, cored and diced
- 80 g/⅔ cup mixed dried berries (sultanas/golden raisins, goji berries, golden berries, cranberries, etc.)

TO SERVE
- 2 tablespoons toasted flaked/ slivered almonds
- 4–5 tablespoons date syrup
- extra oat milk

SERVES 4–6

You might wonder why on earth anyone would want to oven-bake porridge, when it takes so little time to cook the conventional way? Well, it does mean that you can swap standing at the stove and stirring constantly for simply mixing everything together and leaving it to morph into breakfast heaven under its own steam, while you soak in the bath, practice your sun salutations, get ready for work, or even go back to bed with your book!

Preheat the oven to 150°C fan/170°C/325°F/Gas 3.

Mix the oats and oat milk together. Stir in the seeds, vanilla bean paste, ground cinnamon, diced pears and dried berries. Pour everything into a roasting pan, cover with foil and bake for 30 minutes. Remove from the oven and spoon into bowls. Scatter with the toasted almonds and drizzle with date syrup and extra oat milk as desired. Serve at once.

BAY-SCENTED COCONUT MILK BLACK RICE WITH TROPICAL FRUITS

- 3 x 400-ml/14-fl. oz. cans coconut milk
- 250 g/scant 1½ cups riso venere black rice
- 50 g/¼ cup caster/granulated sugar
- a pinch of salt flakes
- 2 bay leaves

TO SERVE
- 1 ripe papaya
- ½ medium ripe pineapple
- 1 ripe mango
- 2 kiwi fruit
- 2–3 passion fruit

SERVES 4

This combination of lightly sweetened chewy black rice and coconut milk is truly amazing – but it does need that pinch of salt flakes to bring everything together, so please don't be tempted to skip it.

Preheat the oven to 150°C fan/170°C/325°F/Gas 3.

Pour the coconut milk into a high-sided roasting pan. Fill up one of the cans with water and add this, and then stir in the rice, sugar, salt and bay leaves. Cover the pan with foil and bake for about 1¼ hours, until the rice is soft and chewy, but not dry.

Peel, then cut the papaya in half, remove the seeds and cut into slices. Peel the pineapple, remove the hard core and cut into chunks. Peel the mango, remove the stone/pit and cut into slices. Peel and slice the kiwi fruit. Cut the passion fruit into halves.

Remove the bay leaves from the rice, give it a stir and serve in bowls, topped with the fruit and a drizzle of passion fruit pulp.

CINNAMON SPICED BRUSCHETTA WITH BROWN SUGAR PLUMS

- 600 g/21 oz. plums, halved and stoned/pitted
- 4 medium slices rye sourdough bread
- 50 g/3½ tablespoons coconut oil
- 50 g/¼ cup dark or light muscovado sugar
- 1 teaspoon ground cinnamon
- plant-based yogurt, to serve

SERVES 4

Sticky, cinnamon-spiced plums and crisp, oven-baked bruschetta make a truly exquisite start to the day. A cascade of coconut or soy yogurt (or a cashew nut cream) lifts it right to the top of the ladder of loveliness.

Preheat the oven to 180°C fan/200°C/400°F/Gas 6.

Arrange the plums, cut side up, along one side of a baking sheet. Spread the bread with about half of the coconut oil. Dot the remaining oil over the plums. Mix the sugar and cinnamon together, sprinkle a little over each of the slices of bread and lay them on the other side of the baking sheet. Scatter the remaining cinnamon sugar over the plums. Bake for about 30 minutes, until the bread is crisp and the plums are beautifully soft. Pile the plums onto the bruschetta and serve warm, with yogurt.

Recipe photograph overleaf

GRAINY PORRIDGE THREE WAYS

ALL

- 50 g/½ cup grainy porridge (see below)

OVERNIGHT NO-COOK PORRIDGE

- ¼ teaspoon ground cinnamon
- 100 ml/scant ½ cup almond milk
- a pinch of salt
- 2 tablespoons plant-based yogurt
- 50 g/⅓ cup mixed dried fruit and nuts
- 1 apple, grated, plus extra to finish
- a drizzle of date syrup
- ½ tablespoon nut butter

EARTH BOWL PORRIDGE

- 300 ml/1¼ cups cashew milk
- 30 g/1 oz. chopped dates (plus extra to finish)
- 30 g/scant ¼ cup mixed nuts, chopped
- 2 tablespoons chia seeds
- ½ teaspoon ground cinnamon
- ½ teaspoon raw cocoa powder
- 2 dried pineapple rings, chopped
- 1–2 tablespoons rice malt syrup

BERRIES & ROSE PORRIDGE

- 250 ml/1 cup simple oat milk
- ½ teaspoon ground cinnamon
- 1–2 teaspoons date syrup
- 100 g/3½ oz. frozen berries
- 2 tablespoons cashew butter
- 1–2 tablespoons coconut yogurt
- a few drops of rose water
- a handful of fresh berries
- a few edible rose petals (optional)

SERVES 1

Here are three elegant ways to eat your grainy porridge. The overnight oats combine nut milk with nuts and cinnamon and finish with a nut butter and freshly grated apple for some zing. The earth bowl is nutty and nourishing with dates, spices and dried pineapple. The berries and rose water pair for a beautiful start to the day.

OVERNIGHT NO-COOK PORRIDGE

The night before serving, stir the cinnamon and almond milk into your grainy porridge with a pinch of salt.

The next day, loosen with a little more water if needed. Top with the yogurt, dried fruit and nuts, apple, a drizzle of date syrup and the nut butter.

EARTH BOWL PORRIDGE

Put the grainy porridge into a saucepan with the cashew milk and stir.

Add the dates, nuts, chia seeds, cinnamon and cocoa powder and cook for 5 minutes, stirring occasionally.

Top with the extra chopped dates, dried pineapple and rice malt syrup.

BERRIES & ROSE PORRIDGE

Put the grainy porridge into a saucepan with the oat milk, cinnamon and date syrup. Cook gently for 5 minutes, stirring, until the oats are creamy and cooked. Tip in the frozen berries and cook for 2 minutes or until warmed through. Stir through the cashew butter, coconut yogurt, a few drops of rose water, then spoon into a serving bowl and top with fresh berries and a few rose petals, if using.

GRAINY PORRIDGE

- 200 g/2 cups rolled/old-fashioned oats
- 200 g/2 cups spelt flakes
- 200 g/2 cups rye flakes

SERVES 8–10

Working in batches, toast the oats, spelt flakes and rye flakes in a large, dry frying pan/skillet for 5 minutes until golden, then leave to cool and store in an airtight container. When you want to eat it, simply combine 50 g/½ cup of the porridge mixture in a saucepan with 300 ml/1¼ cups milk or water. Cook for 5 minutes, stirring occasionally.

TOFU SCRAMBLE

- 150 g/2 cups fresh shiitake mushrooms
- 4 tablespoons olive oil
- 120 g/1 cup onions sliced into thin half-moons
- ½ teaspoon sea salt
- 80 g/1 cup trimmed asparagus, sliced diagonally at the bottom (if using wild asparagus, then only use the soft tops)
- 2 tablespoons tamari
- ½ teaspoon ground turmeric
- 300 g/10 oz. fresh tofu, mashed with a fork
- 4 tablespoons water, if necessary
- 1 teaspoon dark sesame oil
- ½ teaspoon dried basil or 2 tablespoons chopped fresh basil
- crushed black pepper

SERVES 2–3

It's impossible to imagine anybody disliking this yummy way of using tofu. It especially appeals to former egg-lovers since it looks and tastes very similar to scrambled eggs. Actually, way better than scrambled eggs! As you can use many different types of vegetables, herbs and spices, this is just one suggestion for springtime, when asparagus (wild and cultivated) is abundant at farmers' markets. Use a big cast-iron wok to make this dish, or a heavy-bottomed frying pan/skillet as an alternative.

Cut the mushrooms in half lengthways, then cut into thinner wedges. Add the olive oil, onions and salt to a wok or frying pan/skillet and sauté over a medium heat briefly, stirring energetically to prevent sticking.

Add the mushrooms, asparagus, tamari and turmeric and continue stirring with two wooden spoons. When the mushrooms have soaked up a bit of tamari, turn up the heat, add the tofu and stir for another 1–2 minutes. The scramble should be uniformly yellow in colour. At this point you can add the water to make the scramble juicy, and continue cooking for a couple more minutes. However, whether you need water or not depends on how soft your tofu was to begin with – softer types are moist and don't need any water at the end of cooking.

Mix in the dark sesame oil and basil, season with pepper and serve warm, with a few slices of toasted homemade bread.

SOUPS & BROTHS

PUMPKIN COCONUT SOUP
WITH WARMING SPICES

- 1 tablespoon avocado or coconut oil
- 1 onion, diced
- 3 garlic cloves, finely chopped
- 2 tablespoons grated fresh ginger
- 1 teaspoon ground cumin
- ½ teaspoon ground cinnamon
- ½ teaspoon cayenne pepper
- ¼ teaspoon ground nutmeg
- a pinch of ground allspice
- 2 carrots, roughly chopped
- 450 g/3½ cups diced pumpkin or 2 x 400-g/14-oz. cans pumpkin or butternut squash purée
- 475 ml/2 cups boiling water
- 400-g/14-oz. can coconut milk (full fat preferably)
- sea salt, to taste
- 135 g/1 cup cooked brown rice, barley or farro, to serve

SERVES 4–6

This spiced soup is a great warmer for the first chilly weeks of autumn/fall. With its slight sweetness, bold spice combination and nutty grains to serve, it feels grounding and cosy while setting itself apart from other plain pumpkin soups. It's really nice served with some fresh coriander/cilantro leaves and a squeeze of fresh lime juice.

In a large saucepan with a lid, heat the oil over a medium heat. Add the onion, season with salt and cook, stirring occasionally, for about 6–8 minutes, until the onion is turning golden.

Add the garlic, ginger, ground cumin, ground cinnamon, cayenne pepper, nutmeg and allspice and cook for 1 minute, stirring everything frequently.

Add the carrots and pumpkin and season with salt. Pour in the boiling water and stir. Cover and cook for about 10 minutes. Remove the lid and simmer for another 10 minutes, until the vegetables are tender.

Turn off the heat and stir in the coconut milk. Blend with a stick blender or in batches in a food processor until smooth. Divide the soup into bowls and serve with a scoop of cooked brown rice, barley or farro in each.

GREEN THAI SOUP

- olive or avocado oil, for frying
- 1 leek, white and light green parts only, thinly sliced
- 2 garlic cloves, finely chopped
- 2 tablespoons Thai green curry paste (check the label to make sure the brand is vegan)
- 1 broccoli crown with stems, chopped into small pieces
- 475 ml/2 cups boiling water
- 1 courgette/zucchini, roughly chopped
- 125 g/1 cup frozen peas
- 2 large handfuls of kale, stems removed and roughly chopped
- 400-g/14-oz. can coconut milk (ideally full fat)
- 5 sprigs of fresh coriander/ cilantro with stems (plus more for serving), roughly chopped
- sea salt, to taste
- cooked brown rice, to serve (optional)

SERVES 3–4

This soup is perfect for using up all your green veg in the fridge. It has Thai spices from the green curry paste, creaminess from coconut milk and it's packed to the brim with fresh vegetables. You can use spinach (fresh or frozen) or Swiss chard in place of kale, or throw in that random kohlrabi that you don't know what to do with – it's all good in this soup. You can either serve this soup mostly puréed, with a helping of brown rice for texture and bulk, or skip the blender and keep it chunky if you prefer.

In a large saucepan with a lid, heat a good glug of oil over a medium-high heat. Add the leek, season to taste with salt and cook, stirring occasionally, for about 5–7 minutes, until the leek has softened.

Add the garlic and fry for another minute. Stir in the curry paste and cook for another minute. Add the broccoli and boiling water to the pan and stir.

Bring to a simmer and add the courgette. Cover the pan and simmer for about 5 minutes until the vegetables are tender.

Stir in the peas and kale, cover, and cook for another 1–2 minutes until the kale has wilted. Turn off the heat and stir in coconut milk (reserving a little to garnish) and coriander.

If blending, use a stick blender or purée in batches in a food processor until mostly smooth.

Served the soup in bowls with extra coriander, a drizzle of the reserved coconut milk and a portion of cooked brown rice, if desired.

SPRING VEGETABLE SOUP

- olive oil, for frying
- 1 onion, finely diced
- 2 leeks, white and light green parts only, thinly sliced into half-moons
- 3 garlic cloves, finely chopped
- 10 sprigs of fresh thyme, leaves removed from stems
- 1 tablespoon finely chopped fresh parsley leaves and stems
- 950 ml/4 cups vegetable stock/broth
- 400-g/14-oz. can white beans, drained and rinsed
- 1 courgette/zucchini, cut into small, bite-sized pieces
- 125 g/1 cup frozen peas, thawed
- 1 carrot, peeled and shaved into ribbons
- 130 g/2 cups kale, stems removed and shredded
- sea salt, to taste
- vegan pesto, to serve

SERVES 4–6

While this soup works on its own, it is delicious served with a scoop of freshly made or store-bought vegan pesto on top. It adds a herbaceous boost that matches up perfectly with the thawing temperatures of springtime.

Heat a thin layer of olive oil in a large saucepan or Dutch oven over a medium heat. Add the onion and leeks, season with salt and cook, stirring occasionally, for 7–8 minutes until softened.

Stir in the garlic, thyme leaves and parsley and cook for 1 minute.

Pour in the vegetable stock, then turn up the heat and bring everything to a boil. Add the beans, then turn down the heat and simmer uncovered for 15 minutes, stirring a few times.

Add the courgette and cook for another 3 minutes until the courgette is tender but not mushy.

Stir in the peas, carrot ribbons and shredded kale and remove from the heat. Let the soup stand for about 5 minutes to let the flavours mingle.

Pour into bowls and serve with a big scoop of pesto stirred into each.

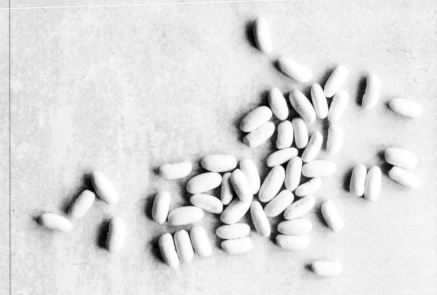

LENTIL, SPINACH & CUMIN BROTH

- 3 tablespoons extra virgin olive oil
- 2 onions, sliced
- 4 garlic cloves, sliced
- 1 teaspoon ground coriander
- 1 teaspoon cumin seeds
- 150 g/¾ cup brown or green lentils
- 1.25 litres/quarts vegetable broth
- 200 g/7 oz. spinach
- freshly squeezed juice of 1 lemon
- sea salt and freshly ground black pepper

TO SERVE
- 4 tablespoons coconut or soy yogurt
- 25 g/1 oz. pine nuts, lightly toasted

SERVES 4

Crispy fried onions are a lovely topping to this Middle Eastern soup, but you have to be brave and really brown them so they look almost black to get the most flavour. In order to do this without burning them, you have to soften them completely to start with.

Heat the extra virgin olive oil in a large, heavy-based saucepan or pot and add the onions. Cook, covered, for 8–10 minutes until softened. Remove half the onion and set aside.

Continue to cook the onion left in the pan for a further 10 minutes until deep brown, sweet and caramelized. Take out and set aside to use for the garnish.

Return the softened onion to the pan and add the garlic, coriander, cumin seeds and lentils and stir for 1–2 minutes until well coated in oil. Add the broth, bring to the boil, then turn down to a gentle simmer for about 30 minutes until the lentils are lovely and soft.

Add the spinach and stir until wilted. Transfer half the soup to a blender and liquidize until you have a purée. Stir back into the soup. Season with lemon juice, sea salt and black pepper.

Divide the soup between serving bowls, add a dollop of yogurt, and scatter the pine nuts and fried onions over the top.

HEALING
MISO BROTH

- 7.5-cm/3-inch piece of dried wakame (seaweed)
- 2.5-cm/1-inch piece of fresh ginger
- 4 spring onions/scallions
- 110 g/²/₃ cup fresh tofu
- 2 tablespoons sesame oil
- 4 garlic cloves, crushed
- a pinch of sea salt
- 500 ml/2 cups hot water
- 1–2 tablespoons barley or rice miso
- 2 tablespoons freshly chopped parsley
- freshly squeezed juice of ½ lemon

SERVES 2

If you want to experiment with the layers of flavours in this nourishing broth, try combining different kinds of miso in the same broth. Since hatcho (soy) miso is of high quality but has a strong taste, try to combine ½ tablespoon of soy miso with ½ tablespoon barley miso to get all the benefits of both kinds of soy paste. In warmer weather, you may want to substitute darker miso pastes with the milder sweet white miso.

Soak the wakame in a bowl with 120 ml/½ cup water until soft. Drain (reserve the water), cut into small pieces and set aside. Peel the fresh ginger and finely dice half of it. Finely grate the other half in a small bowl and keep for later. Chop the spring onions, separate the whites and greens. Cut the tofu into small cubes.

In a frying pan/skillet, sauté the white part of the spring onions for 1 minute in the sesame oil, then add the garlic, ginger and salt. Sauté a little longer, add the hot water, tofu and set-aside wakame and its reserved water and cover. Bring to the boil, then lower the heat and simmer for 4 minutes. Remove from the heat.

Pour about 60 ml/¼ cup hot water into a small bowl. Add the miso and purée really well with a fork, until completely dissolved. Pour back, cover and let sit for 2–3 minutes. Take the grated ginger in your hand and squeeze it to release the juice directly into the hot soup. Discard the remaining ginger pulp. Add the chopped spring onion greens, freshly chopped parsley and lemon juice, and serve immediately.

ONE-POT MISO NOODLE SOUP

- 100 g/3½ oz. dried soba noodles
- 1 teaspoon salt
- ½ tablespoon tamari
- 2½ tablespoons dark sesame oil
- 3 dried shiitake mushrooms
- 1 strip of wakame seaweed (optional)
- 1 tablespoon chopped garlic
- 2 tablespoons chopped fresh ginger
- 1 small onion, diced
- 2 carrots, diced (around 100 g/3½ oz. total weight)
- 120 g/1 generous cup cubed pumpkin
- ¼ teaspoon ground turmeric
- freshly ground black pepper
- a pinch of chilli/chili powder
- 100 g/1½ cups mung bean sprouts
- 2 tablespoons rice or barley miso
- 130 g/4½ oz. spinach leaves, chopped

SERVES 3

A big bowl of this soup makes a great lunch, especially when you feel tired and your energy is low. It's also a great late-night dinner option because it nourishes you but doesn't put too much strain on the already sleepy digestive system. Also, dried shiitake mushrooms have a relaxing effect on the body.

In a large saucepan or pot, boil the noodles in 1.25 litres/quarts of salted water until al dente. Strain, reserving the cooking water. Run the noodles through running cold water, drain, put in a bowl and sprinkle with the tamari and ½ tablespoon of dark sesame oil. Mix well and set aside.

In a small bowl, cover the shiitake and wakame, if using, with hot water and leave to soak.

Rinse the saucepan or pot in which you cooked the noodles and add the remaining dark sesame oil. Over a medium heat, sauté the garlic and ginger for 2–3 minutes, then add the onion, carrots, pumpkin cubes and a pinch of salt. Mix well and sauté for 2–3 minutes.

Add the turmeric, pepper and chilli powder and stir. Once the spices and vegetables start sizzling, add the reserved cooking water and another 500 ml/2 cups hot water. Cover and bring to the boil over a medium heat. Meanwhile, drain the shiitake and wakame and chop finely, discarding the mushroom stems.

Once the soup has started to boil, add the mung beans, shiitake and wakame, lower the heat and cook, covered, for 10 minutes. Put the miso in a small bowl and pour over a ladle of hot soup. Dilute completely with the help of a small whisk or fork. Remove the soup from the heat and add the diluted miso and chopped spinach. Taste and adjust seasoning. Stir, cover and allow to rest for 1 minute.

Divide the cooked noodles among bowls and pour over the soup, making sure that each portion gets a lot of veggies and sprouts. Serve immediately.

SWEET POTATO, CORIANDER & MAPLE SOUP

- 1 litre/quart vegetable stock
- 500 g/1 lb. 2 oz. sweet potatoes, peeled and chopped
- 50 g/2 oz. fresh coriander/cilantro, plus extra to garnish
- 40 ml/2½ tablespoons pure maple syrup
- 40 ml/2½ tablespoons soy sauce
- freshly squeezed juice of 2 limes
- sea salt and freshly ground black pepper

SERVES 4

Sweet potato is a perfect vegetable for soup as it has a smooth, silky and creamy texture. This soup is packed with sweet and salty flavours. If you are serving to anyone who cannot eat gluten, make sure that the soy sauce you use is gluten-free, as not all brands are. This is a 'simmer' soup and needs no cooking steps other than putting everything in a pot to simmer – the ultimate one-pan soup!

Place the vegetable stock in a saucepan and add the peeled sweet potatoes and half of the coriander. Simmer until the sweet potato is soft.

Add the maple syrup, soy sauce and lime juice and season with salt and pepper to taste. Add the remaining coriander and blitz in a blender or food processor until the soup is smooth, or use a stick blender.

Pour the soup into four bowls, garnish with a little fresh coriander and serve straight away.

THREE BEAN SOUP

- 1 tablespoon olive oil
- 1 onion, chopped
- 1 garlic clove, finely chopped
- 1 yellow (bell) pepper, deseeded and cut into small pieces
- 1 carrot, peeled and cut into small pieces
- 1 courgette/zucchini, cut into small pieces
- 400-g/14-oz. can black beans in water, drained and rinsed
- 400-g/14-oz. can cannellini beans in water, drained and rinsed
- 400-g/14-oz. can red kidney beans in chilli/chili sauce
- 400-g/14-oz. can chopped tomatoes
- 1 tablespoon tomato purée/paste
- 250 ml/1 cup vegan red wine
- 1 litre/quart vegetable stock
- 1 teaspoon dried oregano
- a handful of chopped fresh basil, plus extra to serve
- 100 g/3¹/₂ oz. soup pasta
- sea salt and freshly ground black pepper
- freshly grated vegan Parmesan or Cheddar, to serve

SERVES 6

Beans are a great source of protein for anyone on a vegan diet. You can use any beans of your choice for this soup. Canned beans are easy to use because they are already cooked, but you can prepare your own beans, if you prefer, by soaking them overnight and then cooking according to the packet instructions. The chilli/chili sauce with the kidney beans is generally very mild, so if you prefer a spicier heat, add a little chilli/chili powder or some dried chilli/hot red pepper flakes when you add the beans for a fiery kick.

In a large saucepan, heat the olive oil and fry the onion until soft and translucent. Add the chopped garlic and fry until lightly golden brown, then add the chopped pepper, carrot and courgette and fry for a few minutes to soften.

Add the black beans and cannellini beans to the saucepan along with the kidney beans in chilli sauce, chopped tomatoes, tomato purée, red wine, stock, oregano and basil and simmer for about 30 minutes.

Add the soup pasta to the saucepan and simmer for the time stated on the pasta instructions – usually about 8–10 minutes – until the pasta is cooked. Season well with salt and pepper.

Using a stick blender, blender or food processor, blitz the soup quickly – you want to leave most of the soup in chunks, but blending some of the mixture will help thicken the soup. Taste for seasoning, adding more salt and pepper as needed.

Divide the soup between six bowls and serve with freshly grated Parmesan or Cheddar and some extra chopped basil leaves.

SPINACH & NUTMEG SOUP

- 2 tablespoons olive oil
- 1 onion, finely chopped
- 160 g/5½ oz. spinach
- 1 litre/quart vegetable stock
- 250 g/9 oz. white potatoes, peeled and cut into small cubes
- a pinch of grated nutmeg
- 100 ml/⅓ cup plus 1 tablespoon plant-based double/heavy cream
- sea salt and freshly ground black pepper
- Pangrattato (see page 48) or croûtons, to serve (optional)

SERVES 4

Spinach and nutmeg are a delicious combination – the heady smell of nutmeg really does transform this dish. Spinach is full of vitamins and is one of those super greens that are good for you in so many ways. This is such a quick soup to prepare and a great after-work one-pot supper.

Heat the oil in a large saucepan over a medium heat and sauté the chopped onion until soft and translucent. Add the spinach, stock and potatoes to the saucepan and simmer for about 15–20 minutes until the potatoes are soft.

Season with salt and pepper and a good pinch of freshly grated nutmeg. Blitz in a blender or food processor until the soup is smooth, or use a stick blender. Pour back into the saucepan and add the cream to the soup, then heat through gently.

Serve straight away with pangrattato or croûtons, if using.

SUNSHINE SOUP

- 2 whole corn cobs/ears
- 2 tablespoons olive oil
- 1 onion, chopped
- 3 yellow (bell) peppers, deseeded and cut into chunks
- 1 litre/quart vegetable stock
- freshly squeezed juice of 1 lemon
- marigold and cornflower petals, to garnish
- Pangrattato (see below), to serve (optional)

SERVES 4

This is a happy soup – the colour is vibrant yellow and, sprinkled with dried petals, it makes a perfect summer dish. The soup is also light and healthy and good for the soul. If you want to make the soup thicker, add two potatoes when you add the stock, simmer until the potatoes are soft, and then blend.

Using a sharp knife, on a chopping board, slice the kernels from the corn cobs/ears. Add these to a saucepan with the olive oil and onion and cook over a low heat until the onion is soft and translucent. Add the peppers and cook until they are soft. Add the stock and lemon juice and simmer for 15–20 minutes.

Blitz with a blender or food processor, or use a stick blender, then pass through a fine-mesh sieve/strainer or moulin to remove the corn and pepper skins and to make the soup smooth. Put the soup back in the saucepan and heat through again.

Pour the soup into four bowls and garnish with dried marigold and cornflower petals. Serve with pangrattato, if you like.

PANGRATTATO

- 1 slice of dried bread
- olive oil, for drizzling
- sea salt and freshly ground black pepper

MAKES ABOUT 50 G/1¾ OZ.

Blitz the bread to fine crumbs in a food processor. Heat a little olive oil in a frying pan/skillet and add the crumbs. Season with salt and pepper and toast until the breadcrumbs are crisp. Stir all the time to make sure that the crumbs don't burn.

Variations: You can vary this recipe by adding a clove of garlic or some lemon zest to the blender when processing the crumbs.

MISO POTATO SOUP

- 1½ tablespoons vegetable or sunflower oil
- 1 leek, washed and thinly sliced
- 700 g/1½ lb. floury potatoes, peeled and diced
- 1 tablespoon Amontillado sherry (check the label to ensure it is vegan – optional)
- 1 heaped tablespoon brown miso paste
- 1 litre/quart vegetable stock
- 1 teaspoon soy sauce
- 200 g/3 cups brown closed cap mushrooms, thickly sliced
- 1 tablespoon freshly chopped chives
- sea salt and freshly ground black pepper

SERVES 4

Japanese miso paste adds an umami richness to this textured potato soup. Serve it as a tasty first course or enjoy it on its own for a light lunch.

Heat ½ tablespoon of the oil in a large saucepan over a medium heat. Fry the mushrooms until lightly browned, then remove from the pan and set aside.

Add the remaining oil to the pan, add the leek and fry, stirring, until softened. Add the potatoes and mix well. Add the sherry, if using, and cook for 1–2 minutes. Mix in the miso paste.

Pour in the stock and add the soy sauce. Bring to the boil, cover and simmer for 20 minutes until the potatoes have softened. Taste the soup and adjust the seasoning as required with the salt and freshly ground black pepper.

Remove half the soup and blend it until smooth using a stick blender or a jug blender. Return the blended soup to the pan and mix with the remaining soup. Simmer gently to heat through.

Mix the fried mushrooms into the soup. Garnish with the chives and serve at once.

MASSAMAN POTATO SOUP

- 1 tablespoon olive oil
- 1 onion, finely chopped
- 1 garlic clove, finely chopped
- 1 tablespoon massaman curry paste
- 450 g/1 lb. potatoes, peeled and cut into 2.5-cm/1-inch cubes
- 2 tablespoons peanut butter
- 200 ml/³⁄₄ cup coconut milk
- 600 ml/2¹⁄₂ cups vegetable stock
- freshly squeezed juice of 1–2 limes, to taste
- 1 tablespoon pure maple syrup
- sea salt and freshly ground black pepper

TO SERVE
- salted peanuts, finely chopped
- red chilli/chile slices

SERVES 4

Massaman curry is a Thai delight – a mild but flavour-packed curry bursting with peanuts and potatoes and rich with coconut milk. Traditionally a Massaman curry is made with beef, but this vegan version tastes even better.

Heat the olive oil in a saucepan over a gentle heat and sauté the onion until it is soft and translucent and starts to caramelize. Add the garlic and cook for a further few minutes, taking care it does not burn. Add the massaman paste and cook for a further 1–2 minutes.

Add the potatoes, peanut butter, coconut milk and stock and simmer until the potatoes are very soft. The potatoes will break up and the soup will thicken.

Add the lime juice and maple syrup and season with salt and pepper. Although you can blend the soup, it's nice to leave the potatoes in chunks to add texture to the soup.

Pour the soup into bowls and sprinkle with chopped peanuts, chilli/chile slices and some black pepper to serve.

CARIBBEAN SWEET POTATO & COCONUT SOUP

- 2 tablespoons olive oil
- 1 onion, finely chopped
- 2 garlic cloves, finely chopped
- 1 teaspoon jerk paste
- 1 tablespoon tomato purée/paste
- 600–700 g/1 lb. 5 oz.–1 lb. 9 oz. sweet potato, peeled and cut into chunks
- 700 ml/scant 3 cups vegetable stock
- 400-ml/14-oz. can coconut milk
- sea salt and freshly ground black pepper
- toasted strips of coconut, to serve

SERVES 4–6

Jerk paste has the most amazing fiery flavour. It is so versatile and can be used to flavour anything. It can be very fiery, so take care not to add too much, otherwise the soup can be overpoweringly hot.

In a large saucepan, heat the oil over a gentle heat and add the onion. Fry until soft and translucent. Add the garlic and cook for a few minutes until it is lightly golden brown. Add the jerk paste and fry to infuse the flavours. How much you add depends on how hot you like your food. Jerk paste is generally very fiery so take care not to add too much unless you like very hot spices.

Add the tomato purée and the sweet potatoes and cook for a few minutes more, then add the stock and the coconut milk. Simmer until the potatoes are soft; around 20–30 minutes.

Place the soup in a blender or food processor and blend until smooth, or use a stick blender. Season with salt and pepper to taste. Serve hot with toasted coconut and some extra black pepper.

CREAM OF CAULIFLOWER SOUP

- 2 tablespoons extra-virgin olive oil
- 4 garlic cloves, crushed
- 1 onion, chopped
- 1 cauliflower, cut into florets
- 1 potato, peeled and chopped
- 500 ml/2 cups vegetable stock
- 250 ml/1 cup plant-based milk, unsweetened
- 4 tablespoons nutritional yeast (or to taste)
- sea salt and freshly ground black pepper

TO FINISH
- 1 tablespoon oat cream or dairy-free cream
- handful of chives, finely snipped
- handful of pea shoots
- crushed green peppercorns

SERVES 4

Vegan heaven in a bowl! This dreamy plant-based soup contains nutritional yeast, which gives a deliciously savoury, cheesy flavour without the use of dairy.

Heat the oil in a large pan and add the garlic and onion. Cook over a medium-high heat until golden brown. Add the cauliflower, potato, stock and milk and bring to the boil. Cook over a medium-high heat for about 15–20 minutes or until the cauliflower is soft.

Add the nutritional yeast and some salt and pepper, and blend until smooth using a stick blender.

Serve with a swirl of oat cream and a sprinkling of snipped chives, fresh pea shoots and crushed green peppercorns.

Recipe photograph overleaf

DAN DAN CAULIFLOWER SOUP

- 400 g/14 oz. rice noodles
- 300 g/10½ oz. cauliflower, cut into florets
- 1 carrot, peeled and thinly sliced diagonally with a peeler
- 2 courgettes/zucchini, spiralized
- 100 g/¾ cup frozen edamame beans

STOCK
- 1 litre/quart good-quality vegetable stock
- 3 garlic cloves, crushed
- 4-cm/1½-inch piece of fresh ginger, grated
- 3 teaspoons palm sugar/jaggery

STOCK SAUCE
- 3 tablespoons light soy sauce
- 2 tablespoons tahini
- 4 tablespoons black vinegar (not balsamic)
- 2 teaspoons dark soy sauce
- 1 teaspoon kecap manis
- 1 teaspoon chilli/chili oil, plus extra to garnish
- 2 teaspoons sesame oil

TO GARNISH
- sliced spring onions/scallions
- fresh coriander/cilantro leaves
- toasted sesame seeds

SERVES 4

This dan dan noodle soup is a flavour explosion in a bowl. It is also a very healthy meal that you can have on the table in no time at all. Use whatever accompanying vegetables are in season.

Combine all the stock ingredients in a large saucepan and bring to the boil. Meanwhile, mix the stock sauce ingredients together in a small bowl.

When the stock comes to the boil, place the rice noodles in the stock, then 1 minute later, add the cauliflower and carrot. After another 1 minute, remove the pot from the heat and add the rest of the veg and the stock sauce. Mix well, taste and adjust the seasoning, if required, with extra splashes of ingredients from the stock sauce.

Divide the noodles and vegetables between four bowls. Ladle the soup into the bowls over the vegetables and noodles, and garnish with some sliced spring onions, coriander leaves and toasted sesame seeds – plus some extra chilli oil if you can handle the heat!

CURRIES & STEWS

THAI GREEN CAULI CURRY

- 2 tablespoons coconut oil
- 2 tablespoons green curry paste (check the label says it is vegan)
- 1 red onion, sliced
- 4 garlic cloves, crushed
- 200 g/7 oz. tenderstem cauliflower or cauliflower florets
- 1 red (bell) pepper, deseeded and thinly sliced
- 2 purple or normal carrots, peeled and sliced diagonally
- 2 baby pak choi/bok choy, halved
- 100 g/3½ oz. mangetout/ snow peas
- 1 tablespoon palm sugar/jaggery
- 1 tablespoon liquid aminos (or tamari)
- 400-ml/14- fl oz. can coconut milk
- 3 Makrut lime leaves
- freshly squeezed juice of 1 lime
- sea salt and freshly ground black pepper

TO SERVE

- bunch of purple Thai basil
- sambal oelek (optional)
- cooked rice
- lime wedges

SERVES 4

Aromatic, creamy, fresh and zingy, just like a good Thai curry should be. The addition of liquid aminos in place of the traditional fish sauce adds a depth of flavour and extra umami goodness.

In a large pan or wok set over a medium-high heat, heat half the coconut oil, being cautious of it spitting.

Add the curry paste and fry it, stirring it into the coconut oil, for about 1 minute. Turn the heat down, add the onion and cook until the onion is slightly translucent, about 8 minutes.

Add the garlic, stir together, then add the second tablespoon of coconut oil. Add the cauliflower, red pepper, carrots, pak choi and mangetout. Add the palm sugar, liquid aminos (or tamari) and some salt and pepper and stir everything together. Reduce the heat to medium and cook down, stirring, until the carrots are tender-crisp, about 10–15 minutes.

Add the coconut milk and lime leaves, stir and then let it simmer for about 5 minutes. Squeeze the lime juice over, stir and then remove from the heat.

Add the purple Thai basil and stir in the sambal oelek, if using. Serve with rice and lime wedges.

RED LENTIL DAL

- olive oil or coconut oil, for frying
- 2 onions, finely sliced
- 3 garlic cloves, finely chopped
- 2.5-cm/1-inch piece of fresh ginger, grated
- 2 teaspoons ground cumin
- 1 teaspoon ground turmeric
- 1 teaspoon ground coriander
- 1/2 teaspoon garam masala
- 1/4 teaspoon cayenne pepper
- 400-g/14-oz. can chopped tomatoes
- 270 g/1 1/2 cups dried red lentils
- 2 carrots, finely diced
- 120 g/2 cups kale, shredded
- sea salt and freshly ground black pepper, to taste

TO SERVE
- steamed rice
- a pinch of dried chilli flakes/hot red pepper flakes
- freshly chopped coriander/ cilantro
- coconut cream

SERVES 4–6

This is a delicious combination of lentils, canned tomatoes and a bunch of spices from your arsenal – the type of comforting one-pan stew you can throw together on a cold afternoon or evening when you really can't be bothered to leave the house.

Heat enough oil to thinly coat the base of a large saucepan over a medium-high heat. Add the onions, season to taste with salt and cook for about 10–12 minutes, stirring occasionally, until they begin to caramelize. Add a splash of water if the pan gets too dry.

Add the garlic and ginger and cook for another minute. Stir in the spices and cook for 1 more minute. Add the tomatoes and cook until bubbling again, then add 950 ml/4 cups of water and the lentils. Cover with a lid and bring to the boil.

Add the carrots, cover and simmer for about 20–30 minutes until the lentils are starting to break down and the carrots are tender. Stir in some black pepper and the kale.

Turn off the heat, leave the pan covered and allow to stand for 15 minutes before serving with rice, chilli flakes, coriander and a drizzle of coconut cream.

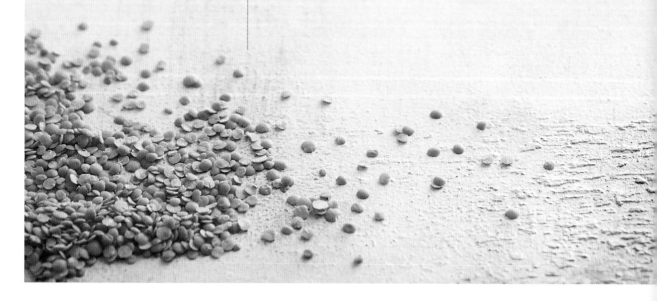

CHICKPEA 'TIKKA' MASALA

- coconut oil, for frying
- 1 onion, finely diced
- 1 yellow (bell) pepper, deseeded and finely chopped
- 2 garlic cloves, finely chopped
- 2 teaspoons garam masala
- 1 teaspoon ground cumin
- ½ teaspoon ground turmeric
- 2 carrots, peeled and finely chopped
- 2 x 400-g/14-oz. cans chickpeas/garbanzo beans, drained and rinsed
- 2 x 400-g/14-oz. cans finely chopped tomatoes in juice or crushed tomatoes
- 400-g/14-oz. can coconut milk (ideally full fat)
- ¼ teaspoon cayenne pepper (optional)
- sea salt, to taste

TO SERVE (OPTIONAL)
- cooked brown rice or quinoa
- vegan naan breads
- freshly chopped coriander/cilantro leaves
- freshly chopped chilli/chile

SERVES 6

The Indian takeout staple gets a vegan makeover with chickpeas/garbanzo beans in a lush tomato-based sauce. Serve with fluffy rice, chopped chilli/chile, fresh herbs and vegan naan breads on the side for a simple and satisfying feast.

Heat enough coconut oil to generously coat the bottom of a large saucepan over a medium-high heat.

Add the onion and pepper and season with salt. Cook, stirring, for about 10 minutes.

Add the garlic and cook for 1 minute. Add the garam masala, cumin and turmeric and continue to cook for another 30 seconds, until fragrant.

Add the carrots, chickpeas and tomatoes. Bring to the boil, then reduce to a simmer and cover with a lid. Simmer for about 15–20 minutes.

Stir in the coconut milk, then simmer for 5 minutes more and remove from the heat. Stir in the cayenne pepper, if using. Let the curry stand, covered with a lid to keep warm, for at least 15 minutes to let the flavours mingle.

Serve over brown rice or quinoa, with vegan naan breads, fresh herbs and chilli, as desired.

TOMATO CURRY

- 1 tablespoon vegetable oil
- 6–8 curry leaves
- 1 teaspoon cumin seeds
- ½ teaspoon ground turmeric
- 400 g/14 oz. tomatoes, each tomato sliced into eight pieces
- 2 teaspoons ground coriander
- ½ teaspoon chilli/chili powder
- 1 teaspoon dark brown sugar
- sea salt and freshly ground black pepper
- fresh coriander/cilantro, to garnish

SERVES 4

Quick and easy to make, this tasty dish is ideal for a super-speedy mid-week meal after a busy day at the office. Serve with steamed basmati rice and an Indian flatbread such as chapati or roti.

Heat the oil in a large, heavy-bottomed frying pan/skillet. Add the curry leaves, cumin seeds and ground turmeric and fry, stirring, for a minute, until very fragrant.

Add the sliced tomatoes and stir to coat with the frying spices. Sprinkle over the ground coriander, chilli powder and sugar, and stir well. Season with salt and pepper.

Continue to cook, stirring often, for 3–5 minutes until the tomato slices are heated through but still retain their shape.

Garnish with fresh coriander and serve at once.

TARKA TOMATO DAL

- 200 g/1 cup split red lentils
- 300 g/10 oz. tomatoes
- 1 tablespoon sunflower oil
- 1 onion, peeled and chopped
- 3 garlic cloves, peeled and chopped
- a 5-cm/2-inch piece of fresh ginger, peeled and chopped
- a handful of curry leaves
- 1 tablespoon tomato purée/paste
- ½ teaspoon ground turmeric
- ½ teaspoon chilli/chili powder
- a pinch of sea salt
- 1 teaspoon brown sugar

TARKA (OPTIONAL)
- 1 tablespoon sunflower oil
- 1 garlic clove, peeled and chopped
- 2 teaspoons cumin seeds

SERVES 4

Tomatoes are excellent paired with earthy pulses; they have an enlivening effect on them. This dish is a classic example of Indian comfort food.

Rinse the lentils under cold, running water, then transfer to a large mixing bowl. Cover with cold water and set aside to soak for 30 minutes.

Scald the tomatoes by pouring boiling water over them in a heatproof bowl. Set aside for 1 minute, then drain and carefully peel off the skins using a sharp knife. Roughly chop, reserving any juices, and set aside.

Heat the oil in a heavy-bottomed saucepan or pot set over a medium heat. Fry the onion, garlic and ginger for 2–3 minutes, stirring often, until softened and fragrant. Stir in the chopped tomatoes, curry leaves, tomato purée/paste, turmeric and chilli powder.

Drain the lentils and add to the pan with 300 ml/1¼ cups of water. Season with salt and stir in the sugar. Bring to the boil, then cover partly, reduce the heat and simmer for 20–30 minutes, stirring often, until the lentils are soft and the water has been absorbed.

When the lentils are cooked, prepare the tarka, if using. Heat the oil in a small frying pan/skillet set over a medium heat. Add the garlic and fry until golden brown. Add the cumin seeds and fry until fragrant. Pour the sizzling tarka over the dal and serve.

LAKSA WITH CAULIFLOWER

- 1 tablespoon vegetable oil
- 4 tablespoons vegan laksa paste
- 1 litre/quart vegetable stock
- 1 tablespoon soy sauce
- 1 tablespoon palm sugar/jaggery
- 400-ml/14-oz. can coconut milk
- 200 g/7 oz. cauliflower, cut into florets or mini cauliflowers
- 80 g/3 oz. mini courgettes/zucchini
- 100 g/3½ oz. asparagus tips
- freshly squeezed juice of 1-2 limes
- 200 g/7 oz. rice/soba noodles

TO FINISH
- 50 g/scant 1 cup beansprouts
- 3 spring onions/scallions, sliced diagonally
- 10 g/½ cup coriander/cilantro, leaves picked
- 1 red chilli/chile, sliced diagonally
- crispy tofu (use leftovers or see recipe right)
- lime wedges
- chilli/chili sauce

SERVES 4

Laksa, the epic Malaysian spicy coconut noodle soup, is a must-try at least once in your life! The soup is rich, fragrant, a bit spicy and loaded with lots of vegetables.

Heat a wok over a high heat and add the oil. Swirl to coat. Add the laksa paste and cook, stirring, for 3 minutes or until fragrant.

Add the stock, soy sauce and palm sugar and bring to the boil. Reduce the heat to medium. Add the coconut milk and simmer for 5 minutes. Add the cauliflower, mini courgettes and asparagus tips, and cook for 2 minutes. Remove from the heat and add the lime juice to taste. Stir to combine.

Meanwhile, place the noodles in a heatproof bowl. Cover with boiling water and leave to stand for 5 minutes or until tender. Drain and divide the noodles between four bowls. Ladle the coconut mixture over the noodles.

Serve with the beansprouts, spring onions, coriander, chilli, crispy tofu, if using, lime wedges and an extra drizzle of chilli sauce.

CRISPY TOFU

- 200 g/7 oz. firm tofu, drained
- 1 tablespoon cornflour/cornstarch
- sea salt
- 2 tablespoons vegetable oil, for frying

SERVES 2–4

Line a plate with a folded paper towel and set the tofu on top. Set a small plate on top of the tofu and weigh it down with something heavy. Pat the tofu dry with more towels. Cut into cubes, season with salt and evenly coat with the cornflour/cornstarch. Heat the oil in a frying pan/skillet and add all of the tofu in a single layer. The tofu should sizzle upon contact – if not, wait a few minutes to let the pan heat up more. At first, the tofu will stick to the pan, so wait until the tofu releases from the pan before browning the next side. Fry until all sides are brown and crispy. Transfer to a cooling rack. It will remain crisp only for a few hours.

MUSHROOM, SPINACH & COCONUT CURRY

- 1 tablespoon sunflower oil
- 1 teaspoon mustard seeds
- 1 onion, finely chopped
- 2.5-cm/1-inch piece of root ginger, finely chopped
- 2 garlic cloves, chopped
- ½ cinnamon stick
- 4 cardamom pods
- 2 teaspoons ground coriander
- 2 teaspoons ground cumin
- ½ teaspoon ground turmeric
- ¼ teaspoon chilli/chili powder
- 400-ml/14-oz. can coconut milk
- 400 g/14 oz. white/cup mushrooms, halved
- 250 g/8 oz. fresh spinach
- sea salt and freshly ground black pepper
- cooked basmati rice, to serve

SERVES 4

If you've come home after a long, busy day and want to make something speedy but tasty for supper, this mellow yet aromatic curry hits the spot! Both mushrooms and spinach require very little cooking, so this is gloriously quick to make. Serve with perfumed basmati rice, naan or paratha flatbreads for a delicious taste of the tropics.

Heat the oil in a casserole dish/Dutch oven or large, heavy saucepan over a medium heat. Add the mustard seeds and fry briefly until they begin to pop. Add the onion, ginger, garlic, cinnamon stick and cardamom pods and fry gently for 5 minutes, stirring often, until the onion has softened and the mixture is fragrant.

Meanwhile, mix together the coriander, cumin, turmeric and chilli powder with 2–3 tablespoons of water to form a spice paste.

Add the spice paste to the onion mixture. Fry, stirring, for 1 minute. Add the coconut milk and stir while bringing to the boil. Add the mushrooms and simmer for 5 minutes. Mix in the spinach and cook briefly until just wilted. Season with salt and pepper and serve at once with rice.

MUSHROOM & BEAN CHILLI

- 1 tablespoon olive oil
- 1 onion, chopped
- 1 garlic clove, chopped
- 1 celery stalk, chopped
- ½ red (bell) pepper, finely chopped
- 150 g/5 oz. field mushrooms (Portabellini), finely chopped
- 1 teaspoon ground cumin
- a pinch of dried oregano
- ½ teaspoon smoked paprika
- 400-g/14-oz. can chopped tomatoes
- 1 teaspoon chipotle paste
- a pinch of sugar
- 400-g/14-oz. can kidney beans, drained and rinsed
- 200 g/6½ oz. button mushrooms, halved if large
- sea salt and freshly ground black pepper

TO SERVE
- freshly chopped coriander/ cilantro
- coconut or soy yogurt
- grated vegan cheese

SERVES 4

This spicy vegan take on a classic chilli con carne is both simple and quick to make. It can also, usefully, be made a day in advance and kept in the fridge until needed. It's especially good with tangy coconut or soy yogurt, which contrasts nicely with this rich tomato-based dish.

Heat the oil over a medium heat in a casserole dish or Dutch oven. Add the onion, garlic, celery and red pepper and fry, stirring, for 5 minutes until softened. Add the field mushrooms, cumin, oregano and smoked paprika and fry, stirring, for 5 minutes.

Add the chopped tomatoes, 200 ml/1 scant cup of water, chipotle paste and sugar. Season with salt and pepper and stir well. Bring to the boil, then stir in the kidney beans and button mushrooms.

Lower the heat to medium and simmer, uncovered, for 15 minutes, stirring now and then. Portion into bowls and garnish with the chopped coriander. Serve with yogurt and grated vegan cheese, if desired.

AUBERGINE TAGINE WITH CORIANDER & MINT

- 2 tablespoons olive oil
- 1 onion, finely chopped
- 2–3 garlic cloves, finely chopped
- 2 red chillies/chile, deseeded and finely chopped
- 2 teaspoons coriander seeds
- 2 teaspoons cumin seeds
- 2 teaspoons sugar
- 1–2 teaspoons ground fenugreek
- 8 baby aubergines/eggplants, with stalks intact
- 2 x 400-g/14-oz. cans chopped tomatoes
- a bunch of fresh mint leaves, roughly chopped
- a bunch of fresh coriander/cilantro, roughly chopped
- sea salt and freshly ground black pepper

SERVES 4

This is a tasty way of cooking the baby aubergines/eggplants that can often be found in Middle Eastern, North African and Asian stores. However, if you can't find them, you can use slender aubergines/eggplants cut into quarters. Serve this dish with a plain or herby couscous.

Heat the oil in the base of a tagine or in a heavy-based saucepan. Stir in the onion, garlic, chillies, coriander and cumin seeds and sugar and sauté for 2–3 minutes, until the onion begins to colour.

Toss in the fenugreek and the aubergines, rolling them in the onion and spice mixture. Tip in the tomatoes, bubble them up, put on the tagine lid and cook over a gentle heat for about 40 minutes, until the aubergines are very tender.

Season the tagine with salt and pepper and toss in most of the mint and coriander. Put the lid back on and cook over a medium heat for a further 5 minutes. Garnish with the rest of the mint and coriander and serve hot.

ROASTED POTATO & FENNEL TAGINE
WITH SUMAC & BALSAMIC VINEGAR

- 2 tablespoons olive oil
- 2 onions, halved lengthways and sliced with the grain
- 2 fennel bulbs, trimmed and finely sliced in their skins (reserve the fronds to garnish)
- 4–6 garlic cloves, smashed in their skins
- 500 g/1 lb. 2 oz. new potatoes, unpeeled, par-boiled for 5 minutes, then sliced (or use leftover cooked potatoes)
- 2–3 tablespoons balsamic vinegar
- 1–2 teaspoons sumac
- a small bunch of fresh flat-leaf parsley, roughly chopped
- sea salt and freshly ground black pepper

SERVES 4

A tagine is the ultimate one-pan dish, bursting with onions and garlic and perhaps a few herbs or spices and is so versatile in terms of what other ingredients you can include. This roasted tagine is delicious served with a fresh tomato or zingy fruit-based salad.

Preheat the oven to 180°C fan/200°C/400°F/Gas 6.

Heat the oil in the base of a tagine or in a heavy-based casserole dish/Dutch oven, stir in the onions and sauté for 3–4 minutes, until they begin to soften and colour. Stir in the fennel and garlic cloves and cook for a further 2–3 minutes. Toss in the potatoes and season with salt and pepper.

Put the tagine in the preheated oven, uncovered, and cook for 35–40 minutes, until the potatoes are golden and slightly roasted.

Toss in the balsamic vinegar and sprinkle the sumac, parsley and fennel fronds over the tagine to serve.

BABY COURGETTE STEW

WITH COURGETTE FLOWERS & LEMON

- 2 tablespoons olive or argan oil
- 2 teaspoons coriander seeds
- 2 garlic cloves, finely chopped
- 1 onion, finely chopped
- 12 baby courgettes/zucchini, trimmed and left whole
- 1 Preserved Lemon (see below), finely sliced
- freshly squeezed juice of 2 lemons
- 4–8 courgette/zucchini flowers, trimmed and left whole
- 1 tablespoon orange blossom water
- sea salt and freshly ground black pepper
- a few fresh mint leaves, finely shredded, to garnish

SERVES 4

A unique spring and early summer dish, this stew is made with baby courgettes/zucchini and the lovely bright yellow flowers of the plant. It is light and lemony and can be served as a first course, as a salad or with a little bit of fresh crusty bread to mop up the juices.

Heat the oil in the base of a tagine or in a heavy-based saucepan, stir in the coriander seeds, garlic and onion and sauté for 1–2 minutes. Toss in the baby courgettes, coating them in the onion and garlic, then add the preserved lemon and lemon juice. Put the lid on the tagine and cook gently for 10–15 minutes, until the courgettes are tender but still have a bite to them.

Season the tagine with salt and pepper, toss in the courgette flowers and splash in the orange blossom water. Put the lid back on and cook gently for 4–5 minutes, until the flowers have wilted in the steam.

Garnish with the mint leaves and serve hot or at room temperature.

PRESERVED LEMONS

- 10 organic, unwaxed lemons, plus the juice of 3–4 lemons
- about 10 tablespoons sea salt
- a large sterilized jar

MAKES A LARGE JAR

Wash and dry the lemons and slice one of the ends off each lemon. Stand each lemon on the flattened end and make two vertical cuts three-quarters of the way through them, as if cutting them into quarters but keeping the base intact. Stuff a tablespoon of salt into each lemon and pack them into the prepared jar. Store the jar of lemons in a cool place for 3–4 days to soften the skins.

After this time, press the lemons down into the jar, so they are even more tightly packed. Pour the lemon juice over the salted lemons, until they are completely covered. Seal the jar and store it in a cool place for at least a month.

To use, rinse the salt off the preserved lemons and pat them dry. Using a small sharp knife, cut the lemons into quarters lengthways and remove all the flesh and pith so that you are just left with the rind. Finely slice or chop the rind according to the recipe.

GREEK SUMMER VEGETABLE STEW
WITH LEMON & OLIVES

- 2 tablespoons olive oil
- 1 onion, chopped
- 500 g/1 lb. 2 oz. small new potatoes (red if available), cubed
- 350 g/12 oz. courgettes/zucchini, halved and quartered lengthways, then sliced thickly
- 3 garlic cloves, sliced
- ¼ teaspoon paprika
- ¼ teaspoon cayenne pepper
- 2 x 400-g/14-oz. cans chopped tomatoes
- leaves from a small bunch of flat-leaf parsley, finely chopped
- sprigs from a small bunch of dill, finely chopped
- 250 g/1½ cups halved fine green beans
- 100 g/¾ cup stoned/pitted cracked green olives
- freshly squeezed juice of ½ a lemon
- sea salt and freshly ground black pepper
- pitta/pita bread, to serve

SERVES 4–6

Any kind of olive can be used here but if you can find some marinated with whole coriander seeds, these are the best ones to use. This is a summer stew and is best eaten lukewarm or at room temperature. Serve with a salad made from cos lettuce dressed with extra virgin olive oil and lemon juice and pitta bread.

Heat the oil in a large saucepan/pot. Add the onion and cook over low heat for 3–5 minutes, until soft. Add the potatoes, courgettes, garlic, paprika, cayenne and a pinch of salt and cook, stirring to coat in the oil, for 1 minute.

Add the tomatoes, parsley and half the dill. Stir to combine and add some water to thin slightly; about 125 ml/½ cup should be enough. Season well, then cover and simmer for 30 minutes.

Add the green beans, cover and continue to simmer for about 20 minutes more, until the beans are tender. Stir in the olives, lemon juice and remaining dill. Taste and adjust the seasoning if necessary. Serve at room temperature with a simple salad and plenty of pitta bread.

BEANS & LENTILS

HARISSA POTATO & LENTIL SALAD

- 100 g/⅔ cup Puy or brown lentils
- 2 tablespoons extra virgin olive oil
- 1 teaspoon freshly squeezed lemon juice
- 400 g/14 oz. waxy potatoes, peeled and finely diced
- 1 red onion, finely chopped
- 1–2 teaspoons harissa paste
- sea salt and freshly ground black pepper
- sunflower oil, for shallow-frying
- freshly chopped coriander/cilantro leaves, to garnish

SERVES 4

The combination of subtly piquant, crispy fried potatoes with the earthy lentils makes this a very satisfying dish and the perfect quick midweek meal to enjoy after a hard day.

Rinse the lentils, drain and place in a large pan. Cover generously with water and bring to the boil. Reduce the heat and simmer for 20 minutes until the lentils are tender but retain some texture, then drain.

Dress the lentils with the olive oil and lemon juice, seasoning well with salt and freshly ground black pepper. Place in a serving dish.

Pour enough sunflower oil into the pan you cooked the lentils in so that it forms a shallow layer across the surface of the pan and heat over a medium heat. Add the diced potatoes and fry, stirring now and then, until golden brown on all sides.

Add the onion and fry for 2–3 minutes until softened. Mix in the harissa, coating the fried potatoes, and fry, stirring, for 2 minutes.

Mix the harissa potatoes with the lentils, sprinkle with coriander leaves and serve.

CREAMY SWEET POTATO & WHITE BEANS

- 1 tablespoon olive oil
- 1 onion, finely diced
- 3 garlic cloves, finely chopped
- 1 large sweet potato, peeled and cut into 1.5-cm/½-inch cubes
- 2 carrots, diced
- 1 tablespoon freshly chopped rosemary leaves
- 3 freshly chopped sage leaves
- 270 g/2 cups cooked white beans, drained and rinsed
- 950 ml/4 cups vegetable stock
- sea salt and freshly ground black pepper, to taste
- roughly chopped fresh parsley, to garnish

SERVES 4–5

White beans lend a creaminess to this stew which, when combined with sweet potato, sage and rosemary, feels like the food version of a cosy sweater. Using canned beans makes this dish possible to be cooked in one pan, whereas using dried beans, would add another stage onto the process. So this is a great recipe to make if you are short on time.

In a large saucepan, heat the olive oil over a medium heat. Add the onion and cook, stirring occasionally, for about 5 minutes, until softened. Add the garlic and cook for 1 minute more. Stir in the sweet potato, carrots, rosemary and sage. Season well with salt and cook for another 2–3 minutes until the herbs are fragrant.

Add the white beans and vegetable stock and bring everything to the boil. Simmer over a medium-low heat, covered with a lid, for 20 minutes until the sweet potato has softened. Uncover, stir and simmer for a final 5 minutes. Crush a few white beans against the side of the pot with a wooden spoon to release their starch and thicken the stew.

Spoon into bowls and garnish with chopped parsley and freshly ground black pepper to serve.

Note: If you wanted to add an extra step (and pan) to this recipe you could use 170 g/1 cup dried white beans instead of the canned. Soak the beans overnight in cold water for at least 8 hours or longer. When you're ready to cook them, drain off the soaking liquid and discard, then put the beans in a medium saucepan and cover with fresh water. Bring to the boil, adding a pinch of salt and any fresh herbs you have lying around (a few thyme sprigs, sage leaves, parsley stems, etc.). Simmer for about 30–40 minutes, or until tender. The cooking time will depend on your beans, how long they were soaked for and how old they are. Drain the beans and then use as above.

CAULIFLOWER, BUTTERNUT SQUASH & CHICKPEAS

- 2 tablespoons flavourless oil
- 2 red onions, sliced
- 4 garlic cloves, crushed
- 4-cm/1½-inch piece each of fresh ginger and turmeric, grated
- 4 cardamom pods, bruised
- 1 lemongrass stalk, bruised
- 2 bird's eye chillies/chiles, halved
- 2 teaspoons garam masala
- 1 teaspoon ground cumin
- 500 g/1 lb. 2 oz. butternut squash, peeled, deseeded and cut into 1-cm/½-inch cubes
- 4 mini cauliflowers or 500 g/ 1 lb. 2 oz. cauliflower, cut into florets
- 2 sprigs of curry leaves
- 400-g/14-oz. can chickpeas/ garbanzo beans, drained and rinsed
- 400-g/14-oz. can chopped tomatoes
- 400-ml/14-oz. can coconut milk
- 10 g/½ cup coriander/cilantro, leaves picked
- freshly squeezed juice of ½ lime, plus extra wedges to serve
- sea salt and freshly ground black pepper
- cooked brown rice and/or vegan naan breads, to serve

SERVES 4

This is a perfect mid-week meal for when you're in need of a little rejuvenation. Super-simple, super-tasty and good for both body and soul.

Place the oil and sliced onions in a wide, deep saucepan and cook over a gentle heat, with the lid on, for 5 minutes, stirring occasionally.

Add the garlic, ginger, turmeric, cardamom pods, lemongrass, chillies, garam masala and cumin, plus a splash of water to stop the pan from going dry, and cook the paste for a minute.

Add the chopped butternut squash and mini cauliflowers or cauliflower florets, plus the curry leaves, chickpeas and canned tomatoes. Add the coconut milk and a little salt and pepper. Stir everything together and bring to the boil, then turn down the heat and cover with a lid.

Cook for 20–25 minutes until the vegetables are cooked through and the sauce has thickened. Add a splash more water if the pan gets too dry.

Add the coriander and lime juice and serve with brown rice and/or vegan naan breads and lime wedges.

ONE-POT CHICKPEA, CHARD & POTATO

- 2 tablespoons olive oil
- 1 onion, chopped
- 1 celery stalk, thinly sliced
- 1 red (bell) pepper, deseeded and chopped into short strips
- 1 teaspoon sweet smoked pimentón or paprika
- a splash of vegan dry white wine
- 300 g/10½ oz. waxy potatoes, quartered
- 400 ml/1¾ cups vegetable stock
- 400-g/14-oz. can chickpeas/ garbanzo beans, drained and rinsed
- 200 g/7 oz. chard or spinach, shredded
- 1 tablespoon chopped preserved lemon (see page 80, optional)
- sea salt and freshly ground black pepper

SERVES 4

This is a homely, nourishing one-pot meal. The potatoes soak up the stock, becoming tasty and tender, contrasting well with the nutty chickpeas/garbanzo beans and the chard.

Heat the olive oil in a frying pan/skillet. Add the onion and fry gently over a low heat for 5 minutes, stirring often. Add the celery and red pepper and fry for a further 3 minutes.

Sprinkle over the pimentón and add the white wine. Cook briefly, stirring, then add the potatoes and stock. Season with salt and freshly ground black pepper.

Bring to the boil, cover, reduce the heat and simmer for about 10 minutes. Add the chickpeas and cook for a further 10 minutes until the potatoes are tender.

Add the chard or spinach and mix well. Cover and cook for 5 minutes, until the chard has wilted and softened. Mix in the preserved lemon (if using) and serve at once.

MOROCCAN-SPICED LENTILS

- olive oil, for frying
- 1 small red onion, finely diced
- 1 yellow (bell) pepper, deseeded and finely diced
- 2 tablespoons tomato purée/paste
- 2 teaspoons sweet smoked paprika
- 1 teaspoon ground cumin
- ½ teaspoon ground coriander
- 2 garlic cloves, finely chopped
- 2 x 400-g/14-oz. cans crushed or chopped tomatoes in juice
- a pinch of saffron threads (optional)
- 160 g/¾ cup dried black or French/du Puy lentils, soaked for an hour or overnight, drained and cooked (see Note right)
- large handful of fresh baby spinach, roughly chopped
- 1 tablespoon harissa
- 1 tablespoon agave syrup
- sea salt, to taste

TO SERVE
- freshly chopped parsley or coriander/cilantro
- toasted vegan flatbread, pitta/pita or naan breads

SERVES 4–5

This richly spiced tomato-based dish is easy enough to put together on a weeknight and leftovers make a great lunch the next day. Try serving this with warm pitta breads.

Heat a thin layer of oil in a large frying pan/skillet with high sides and a lid or in a casserole dish/Dutch oven over a medium heat. Add the onion and pepper, season with salt and sauté for about 4–6 minutes until the onion is translucent.

Stir in the tomato purée and cook for 1 minute. Add the spices and garlic and cook for 30 seconds more. Stir in the tomatoes and saffron (if using). Cover with a lid and simmer over a medium-low heat for 15 minutes.

Add the cooked and drained lentils to the tomato mixture and cook, uncovered, for another 10 minutes, until the liquid has slightly reduced.

Stir in the spinach and let it wilt. Remove from the heat and stir in the harissa and agave syrup. Serve warm scattered with freshly chopped herbs and pitta bread to mop up the sauce.

Note: To cook the lentils, put them in a medium saucepan with 710 ml/3 cups of water and a pinch of salt. Bring to the boil, then reduce the heat to medium-low, cover with a lid and cook for about 18–20 minutes. You want them al dente with a little bit of bite. When cooked, drain the lentils in a colander/strainer. Alternatively, use a can or pouch of ready-cooked lentils to make this even simpler.

BUTTERNUT SQUASH & BLACK BEAN CHILLI

- avocado or olive oil, for frying
- 1 onion, diced
- 375 g/3 cups peeled butternut squash, cut into small 1.5-cm/½-inch cubes
- 2 tablespoons tomato purée/paste
- 1 large garlic clove, finely chopped
- 3 teaspoons ground cumin
- 2 teaspoons smoked paprika
- ¼ teaspoon ground cinnamon
- ¼ teaspoon cayenne pepper
- 400-g/14-oz. can crushed or chopped tomatoes in juices
- 2 x 400-g/14-oz. cans black beans in their liquid
- sea salt, to taste

TO SERVE (OPTIONAL)

- diced avocado or Avocado Dip (see opposite)
- vegan sour cream
- chopped large spring onions/green onions
- corn chips

SERVES 4–6

Cubes of butternut squash and black beans make this dish hearty and satisfying. It's a perfect Sunday afternoon batch-cooking recipe to make enough for leftovers to eat throughout the week. The flavours deepen when it has time to sit, so it tastes even better the next day.

In a large saucepan with a lid, heat enough oil to cover the base of the pan over a medium heat.

Add the onion, season with salt and cook for about 5 minutes until translucent. Add the butternut squash and cook, stirring occasionally, for 5 minutes.

Add the tomato purée, stir and cook for 1 minute. Add the garlic, cumin, paprika, cinnamon and cayenne pepper and cook for 1 minute more. Pour in the tomatoes and black beans along with the liquid from the cans. Season with salt and reduce the heat to medium-low.

Cook covered for about 30 minutes, stirring occasionally, until the butternut is tender. You may need to add 120 ml/½ cup or more water, if the chilli becomes too dry or thick for your liking. Serve with your desired toppings.

AVOCADO DIP

- 1 avocado, peeled and stoned/pitted
- freshly squeezed juice of half a lemon or lime
- a small handful of fresh coriander/cilantro leaves
- sea salt, to taste

MAKES 175–235 ML/¾–1 CUP

Place the avocado, lemon or lime juice, coriander leaves and a good pinch of sea salt in a food processor or blender. Blend to a smooth purée.

Add water a tablespoon at a time and blend again until you reach the desired consistency – thick enough for a dip but thin enough to drizzle. Taste and add extra sea salt, if desired.

EASY BAKED LENTILS & ROOT VEG

- 1 onion, sliced
- 2 garlic cloves, peeled and chopped
- 4 tablespoons olive oil
- 2 tablespoons Berbere Spice Mix (see below)
- 2 large carrots
- 1 large sweet potato (about 250 g/9 oz.), peeled and cut into bite-sized chunks
- 400-g/14-oz. can chopped tomatoes
- 4-cm/1½-inch piece of fresh ginger root, grated
- 450 g/15 oz. passata/strained tomatoes
- 800 ml/generous 3¼ cups well-flavoured vegetable stock
- 2 tablespoons good-quality tomato ketchup
- 150 g/scant 1 cup dried red lentils, rinsed
- a large handful of fresh baby spinach leaves
- a bunch of freshly chopped parsley
- chilli/chile oil, to serve (optional)

SERVES 4

This Ethiopian-influenced lentil dish is great when you're craving something fuss-free and filling but full on flavour. Try not to frown at the idea of adding tomato ketchup to tomato-based dishes – good-quality tomato ketchup puts back the sweetness that can often be lacking in canned tomatoes and passata/strained tomatoes.

Preheat the oven to 170°C fan/190°C/375°F/Gas 5. Scatter the onion over the base of a deep roasting pan. Add the garlic to the pan, drizzle everything with the olive oil and scatter over the berbere spice mix. Give it a good stir to coat everything in the spice mix and cook for 10 minutes.

Cut the carrots into triangular-shaped chunks. Remove the roasting pan from the oven and toss in the carrots and sweet potato. Pour in the chopped tomatoes and stir in the grated ginger. Add the passata, stock and tomato ketchup. Stir in the lentils, cover with foil and cook for 30–35 minutes, until the vegetables and lentils are soft and the casserole is nicely thickened.

Stir in the spinach leaves and half of the parsley, and return the pan to the oven for a further 3–4 minutes. Serve with an extra scattering of chopped parsley, and chilli oil, if desired.

BERBERE SPICE MIX

- 2 tablespoons dried chilli/hot red pepper flakes
- 1½ teaspoons flaked sea salt
- 1½ teaspoons coarsely ground black pepper
- 1½ teaspoons ground cumin
- 1½ teaspoons coriander seeds
- ½ teaspoon fenugreek powder
- ½ teaspoon ground ginger
- ⅓ teaspoon allspice
- ⅓ teaspoon ground cloves
- ⅓ teaspoon ground nutmeg
- seeds from 2 green cardamom pods

MAKES ABOUT 75 G/2¾ OZ.

Grind the spices together using a pestle and mortar, until you have a lightly textured powder. Store in an airtight container.

ADZUKI BEANS
WITH AMARANTH

- 200 g/1 cup dried adzuki beans
- 180 g/1½ cups peeled, seeded and cubed Hokkaido or kabocha pumpkin
- 70 g/⅓ cup amaranth
- 2 tablespoons soy sauce
- ½ tablespoon umeboshi vinegar
- ½ teaspoon ground turmeric
- ½ teaspoon sea salt

SERVES 2–3

This nourishing dish is made with only a few ingredients, and is rich and creamy with slight hint of sweetness.

Cover the adzuki beans with 1 litre/quart water in a saucepan and soak overnight (this is not necessary but will speed up the cooking). Bring them to a boil in the soaking water, then add the pumpkin and cook, half-covered, over a low heat for about 30 minutes until the adzuki beans are half-done.

Add the amaranth and cook until both the adzuki beans and amaranth are soft (another 20–30 minutes). Season with the remaining ingredients and adjust the thickness by adding hot water, if necessary.

CAULIFLOWER, VEGETABLE & BEAN RAGÙ

- 2 onions, diced
- 2 carrots, diced
- 2 celery sticks, diced
- 2 heads of cauliflower, cut into florets
- 1 large aubergine/eggplant, diced
- 2 tablespoons olive oil
- a few sprigs each of fresh thyme, rosemary and sage
- 2 fresh bay leaves
- 100 ml/⅓ cup vegan red wine
- 2 x 400-g/14-oz. cans good-quality plum tomatoes
- 400-g/14-oz. can haricot/navy beans, drained and rinsed
- sea salt and freshly ground black pepper

MAKES 2.5 KG/5½ LB.

This will become your staple tomato ragù. Keep a batch in the freezer ready to add to your chilli, swirl through pasta or serve instead of home-made baked beans for brunch.

Place the onions, carrots, celery, cauliflower and aubergine in a large, flameproof casserole dish/Dutch oven with the olive oil. Cook over a medium heat for 20 minutes, or until softened, stirring often, as the veg sticks easily.

Tie the herb sprigs and bay leaves together with string/twine to make a bouquet garni and add to the pan. After a few minutes, pour in the wine and leave to bubble and cook away for about 3–5 minutes.

Tip in the tomatoes, breaking them up with the back of a wooden spoon, then pour in two cans of water. Cook for 30 minutes, then add the beans. Cook for 30 minutes more, or until thickened and reduced, stirring and mashing occasionally with a potato masher, and adding splashes of water to loosen, if needed.

Season to taste with salt and pepper before serving.

Recipe photograph overleaf

SWEET POTATO, SPINACH & CHICKPEAS
WITH COCONUT

- 1 tablespoon vegetable oil
- 1 onion, halved and sliced
- 30-g/1 oz. piece of fresh ginger, peeled and grated
- 1–2 fresh red chillies/chiles, halved and sliced
- 1 teaspoon curry powder
- 1 teaspoon ground cumin
- 1.3 kg/3 lb. sweet potatoes, peeled and cubed
- 400-ml/14-oz. can coconut milk
- 450 ml/scant 2 cups vegetable stock
- 400-g/14-oz. can chickpeas/garbanzo beans, drained and rinsed
- 225 g/8 oz. fresh baby spinach leaves, washed
- sea salt
- jasmine rice, to serve

SERVES 4–6

This falls somewhere between a stew and a soup and is delicious served with fragrant jasmine rice. If you like things spicy, add two chillies/chiles and all their seeds; if not, add one and keep the seeds out. It will be very mild and the specks of red are pretty against the orange tones of the dish.

Heat the oil in a large saucepan/pot. Add the onion and cook over a low heat for 3-5 minutes, until soft. Add the ginger, chillies, curry powder, cumin and a pinch of salt. Cook for 1-2 minutes, stirring, until aromatic.

Add the sweet potatoes and stir to coat in the spices. Add the coconut milk and stock and a little water if necessary, just to cover the sweet potatoes; the mixture should be soupy as it will cook down. Bring to the boil, then simmer, uncovered, for 15 minutes.

Add the chickpeas and continue to simmer for about 15-20 minutes more, until the sweet potatoes are tender.

Add the spinach, in batches, stirring to blend and waiting for each batch to wilt before adding the next. Taste and adjust the seasoning if necessary. Serve immediately with jasmine rice.

RICE & GRAINS

CAULIFLOWER LARB WITH COCONUT RICE & FRESH LEAVES

- 30 g/¾ cup coconut chips
- 3 tablespoons vegetable oil
- 1 large cauliflower, finely chopped
- 1 lemongrass stalk, tough outer layers removed, finely chopped
- 4 fresh Makrut lime leaves, thinly sliced
- 3 green Thai chillies/chiles, finely chopped
- 4 tablespoons soy sauce
- freshly squeezed juice of 1 lime
- 5 spring onions/scallions, thinly sliced
- 10 g/½ cup fresh coriander/cilantro, leaves picked and chopped
- 10 g/½ cup fresh mint, leaves picked and chopped
- sea salt

TO SERVE
- lettuce leaves
- cooked jasmine rice
- purple basil (optional)

SERVES 4

Larb is a flavoursome dish from Northern Thailand that is usually made with meat and served as a salad with rice and crisp leaves. This is a fragrant, sweet and tangy cauliflower version.

Heat a wok or a large, heavy-based frying pan/skillet over a medium-high heat. Add the coconut chips and cook, stirring, for 2 minutes or until golden brown. Remove from the heat. Transfer to the bowl of a food processor and process until finely ground. Set aside.

Heat the oil in the same wok or frying pan/skillet over a high heat. Add the cauliflower, lemongrass, lime leaves, chillies, soy sauce and lime juice and cook, stirring occasionally, for 5 minutes or until the cauliflower changes colour. Transfer to a heatproof bowl and set aside for 15 minutes to cool.

Toss the spring onions, coriander and mint into the cauliflower mixture. Season with salt. Serve with lettuce leaves and cooked jasmine rice mixed with the finely ground toasted coconut. Garnish with purple basil, if you like.

GREEN KITCHARI BOWL

- 180 g/1 cup dried yellow split peas or lentils
- 90 g/½ cup long grain brown or jasmine rice
- 2–3 tablespoons coconut oil
- 1 tablespoon grated fresh ginger
- 2 teaspoons ground cumin
- 1 teaspoon ground coriander
- 1 teaspoon fennel seeds
- 1 teaspoon ground fenugreek
- 1 teaspoon ground turmeric
- 1.2 litres/quarts water or vegetable stock
- 1 crown broccoli, cut up very small into an almost rice-like texture
- 1 medium courgette/zucchini, trimmed and coarsely grated
- 60 g/1 packed cup baby spinach or baby kale, roughly chopped
- sea salt

TO SERVE
- freshly chopped coriander/cilantro
- Garlic Yogurt Dip (see right, optional)

SERVES 4–6

Kitchari is a very simple combination of rice, lentils or split peas and spices – but the result is something wholesome and deeply comforting, kind of like an Indian-spiced risotto.

Rinse the yellow split peas or lentils and rice in a colander/strainer under cold water until the water runs clear.

In a large saucepan over a medium-high heat, heat enough coconut oil to cover the base of the pan. Add the ginger and cook, stirring, for 30 seconds. Add the spices, season with salt and cook for another 30 seconds, until fragrant.

Add the lentils and rice and stir to coat in the spices. Pour in the water or vegetable stock and bring to the boil.

Reduce the heat to medium-low, cover with a lid and simmer for 35–45 minutes, stirring occasionally, until the rice and lentils are tender but not mushy and most of the liquid has been absorbed. (You may need to add a little more liquid if the mixture becomes too dry.)

Stir in the broccoli. Cover and cook for another 4–5 minutes. Stir in the courgette and spinach or kale, then remove from the heat and leave to stand for 5 minutes. Serve warm scattered with freshly chopped coriander and garlic yogurt dip, if desired.

GARLIC YOGURT DIP

- 215 g/1 cup plain unsweetened vegan yogurt
- 1 garlic clove, finely grated
- ¼ teaspoon salt
- black pepper, to taste
- 1 tablespoon olive oil, plus more to serve

In a small bowl, stir together the dip ingredients with a fork. Serve with additional olive oil and freshly ground black pepper, if desired.

MAKES ABOUT 235 ML/1 CUP

ARTICHOKE & BROAD BEAN PAELLA

- 4 medium artichokes, halved or quartered
- 1 lemon, halved
- 4 tablespoons extra virgin olive oil
- 2 bay leaves, bruised
- 4 garlic cloves, crushed
- 1 onion, finely chopped
- 1.2 litres/quarts hot vegetable stock
- 250 g/2 cups shelled and peeled broad/fava beans
- 350 g/scant 2 cups bomba, Calasparra or arborio rice
- 2 tablespoons freshly chopped mint
- sea salt and freshly ground black pepper
- vegan garlic mayonnaise or saffron aioli, to serve

SERVES 4

Fresh artichokes are best used here if you can get hold of them. This recipe has been adapted to include freshly chopped mint and, unusually for paella, to serve it with a vegan garlic mayo or saffron aioli – it just seems to work.

Start by preparing the artichokes. Cut the stems off to about 2 cm/³⁄₄ inch and the leaves down to about 3–4 cm/1¼–1½ inch from the top. Peel away and discard any tough leaves to reveal the round base. In the centre there will be a hairy 'choke'. Scoop this out and discard it. Cut the bases in half and put them into a bowl filled with cold water. Squeeze in the juice from both lemon halves, and put the squeezed halves in the water too.

Heat the oil in a 35-cm/14-inch paella pan (or shallow flameproof casserole dish/Dutch oven) and add the bay leaves. Fry gently for 30 seconds, until fragrant, and then stir in the garlic, onion and a little salt and pepper. Lower the heat and cook for 20 minutes, until the onion is caramelized. Add the artichoke halves and stock, bring to the boil and simmer gently for 10 minutes.

Stir in the broad beans, rice and mint and simmer gently for 20 minutes, until the rice is al dente and the liquid absorbed. Let sit for 10 minutes before serving with a bowl of saffron aioli.

Tip: To make individual paellas, follow the above method until you have added all the ingredients except the aioli. Combine everything and then divide between 4 individual pans. Bake in an oven preheated to 180°C fan/200°C/400°F/Gas 6 for about 20 minutes, until the rice is cooked.

VEGETABLE PAELLA

- 25 g/scant ¼ cup blanched almonds, toasted
- 4 tablespoons roughly chopped fresh parsley
- 4 garlic cloves
- 6 tablespoons extra virgin olive oil
- 750 g/1 lb. 10 oz. baby vegetables, such as carrots, turnips, fennel, courgettes/zucchini and green beans
- 1 litre/quart hot vegetable stock
- 150 g/1¼ cups fresh or frozen peas (thawed if frozen)
- 1 large leek, trimmed and thinly sliced
- 1 green (bell) pepper, seeded and finely chopped
- 1 plum tomato, peeled and finely chopped
- 2 teaspoons sweet paprika
- ¼ teaspoon saffron threads, ground
- 350 g/scant 2 cups bomba, Calasparra or arborio rice
- sea salt and freshly ground black pepper
- courgette/zucchini flowers, sliced, to garnish (optional)

SERVES 4–6

Paella is the ultimate one-pan rice dish. This particular version has a pesto-like sauce added to it, made with ground almonds, garlic and parsley. A selection of baby vegetables have been used here, but really any vegetable works well.

Pound the toasted almonds in a pestle and mortar (or use a food processor) with the parsley and 2 of the garlic cloves, until finely ground. Stir in 2 tablespoons of the oil. Set aside.

Trim the baby vegetables and halve any larger ones. Bring the stock to a boil a 35-cm/14-inch paella pan (or shallow flameproof casserole dish/Dutch oven) and blanch the baby vegetables and the peas for 1–3 minutes, depending on their size. Drain and reserve the stock in a jug.

Heat the remaining oil in the same pan that you blanched the vegetables in. Crush the remaining garlic and add it to the pan with the leek, green pepper and some salt and pepper. Fry gently for 10 minutes, until lightly golden. Add the tomato, paprika and ground saffron, and cook for a further 8–10 minutes, until the sauce is dry and sticky.

Stir the rice and parsley pesto into the pan, until the rice grains are well coated. Pour in the reserved stock, bring to the boil and simmer gently for 15 minutes, then stir in the blanched vegetables and continue to cook for a further 5–8 minutes, until the rice is al dente, the stock absorbed and the vegetables are tender. Season with salt and pepper. Leave to sit for 10 minutes before serving. Garnish with sliced courgette flowers, if you like.

PERSIAN-STYLE SAFFRON RICE
WITH POTATOES

- 250 g/1⅓ cups basmati rice
- 1 teaspoon saffron threads, finely ground or 1 teaspoon saffron powder
- 2 tablespoons hot water
- 4 tablespoons sunflower or vegetable oil
- 1 onion, finely chopped
- 200 g/7 oz. waxy potatoes, peeled and diced into 1-cm/½-inch cubes
- 2 tablespoons dried barberries or currants
- 1 tablespoon pine nuts
- 15 g/1 tablespoon plant-based spread
- 1 teaspoon ground cinnamon
- sea salt

SERVES 6

Fragrant with spices, this textured pilaff made from long-grained basmati is an elegant one-pan rice dish, perfect for entertaining. Serve with vegetable kebabs/kabobs or a roast aubergine/eggplant salad for a Middle Eastern-inspired feast.

Rinse the basmati rice 2–3 times to wash out excess starch. Cover in cold water and set aside to soak for 45 minutes.

Mix the ground saffron with the hot water and set aside to infuse.

Heat the oil in a heavy-based saucepan. Add the onion and fry gently over a low heat, stirring now and then, for 5 minutes until softened. Add the potato cubes, increase the heat to medium and fry, stirring often, for 8 minutes, until lightly browned. Add the barberries or currants and pine nuts and fry, stirring, for 2 minutes.

Add the plant-based spread. Once it has melted, add the ground cinnamon, mixing well.

Drain the soaked rice and add to the pan, mixing well. Add 300 ml/1¼ cups water, the saffron liquid and the salt and bring to the boil. Cover, reduce the heat and cook over a very low heat for 15 minutes until the water has been absorbed and the rice is tender. Serve at once.

BEAN & PEA PAELLA WITH MINT SALSA VERDE

- 60 ml/4 tablespoons olive oil
- 2 garlic cloves, crushed
- 2 tomatoes, seeded and finely chopped
- 2 teaspoons sweet paprika
- ¼ teaspoon saffron threads
- 350 g/1¾ cups arborio rice
- 900 ml/scant 4 cups vegetable stock
- 150 g/5½ oz. green beans, trimmed and halved
- 150 g/1 heaping cup shelled broad/fava beans
- 150 g/1 cup shelled peas
- 50 g/½ cup stoned/pitted black olives
- sea salt and freshly ground black pepper
- lemon wedges and vegan aïoli, to serve

MINT SALSA VERDE
- 1 bunch of fresh mint (about 30 g/1 oz.)
- ½ bunch of fresh flat-leaf parsley (about 15 g/½ oz.)
- 1 garlic clove, chopped
- 1 tablespoon capers, drained and washed
- 1 teaspoon Dijon mustard
- 2 teaspoons white wine vinegar
- 150 ml/⅔ cup extra virgin olive oil

SERVES 4–6

This is the perfect summer rice dish with its multitude of beans and peas rounded off with a piquant minty herb salsa. It is a great al fresco sharing dish, and would be delicious served with a tofu-based aïoli.

Heat the oil in a 3-litre/quart flameproof casserole dish/Dutch oven over a medium heat, add the garlic and fry for 30 seconds or until it starts to soften (be careful not to let it burn). Add the tomatoes, paprika, saffron and a little salt and pepper and cook for about 5 minutes until the tomatoes and oil start to separate.

Scatter the rice over the tomato mixture, stir well and cook for 2 minutes. Add the stock, bring to the boil and cook, uncovered, over a medium-low heat for 10 minutes. Scatter both types of beans and the peas over the top of the rice, cover the pan and cook for a further 10–15 minutes until the rice is tender, the vegetables cooked and the stock absorbed.

Meanwhile, make the salsa verde. Place all the ingredients in a food processor or blender with some salt and pepper. Purée to form a smooth paste. Adjust the seasonings to taste.

Remove the pan from the heat, scatter over the olives, then cover with a clean tea/dish towel and leave to sit for 5 minutes. Drizzle over some of the salsa verde and serve with lemon wedges and aïoli, if wished.

BAKED RICE
WITH CHICKPEAS & RAISINS

- 5 tablespoons olive oil
- 1 head garlic, trimmed but left whole
- 1 small onion, finely chopped
- 1 large tomato, finely chopped
- 1 teaspoon sweet paprika
- ½ teaspoon ground cinnamon
- 200 g/1½ cups cooked chickpeas/garbanzo beans, drained and rinsed
- 100 g/⅔ cup (dark) raisins
- 1 litre/quart vegetable stock
- 350 g/scant 2 cups bomba, Calàsparra or arborio rice
- sea salt and freshly ground black pepper

TO SERVE
- freshly chopped parsley
- vegan garlic mayo or saffron aioli

SERVES 4–6

Here rice is combined with chickpeas/garbanzo beans and raisins, as is typical of the sweet/savoury nature of many Moorish recipes, which lend themselves particularly well to this baked rice dish.

Preheat the oven to 180°C fan/200°C/400°F/Gas 6. Heat the oil in a flameproof casserole dish/Dutch oven. Fry the head of garlic over a medium heat for 5 minutes, until golden. Add the onion and lower the heat, fry gently for 10 minutes, then add the tomato, paprika and cinnamon, and cook for a further 5–8 minutes, until the sauce is quite dry. Season with salt and pepper.

Stir in the chickpeas, raisins and stock, and bring to the boil. Sprinkle over the rice, stir once and return to the boil. Transfer to the oven. Bake for about 25 minutes, until the rice is al dente and the stock absorbed. Remove from the oven and leave to sit for 10 minutes before serving with the aioli.

Tip: To make a tasty vegetable stock place roughly chopped onions, carrots, leeks, garlic, mushrooms and potatoes in a large pan, as well as some roughly chopped parsley and thyme, and some salt and pepper. Add 2 litres/quarts water, bring to the boil, then lower the heat and simmer for 45 minutes, until the stock has taken on a good flavour. Strain and reserve the stock.

CAULIFLOWER RISOTTO

- 2 tablespoons olive oil
- 1 onion, finely chopped
- 250 g/1⅓ cups risotto rice
- a big pinch of saffron threads
- 90 ml/⅓ cup vegan dry white wine
- 900 ml–1 litre/quart hot vegetable stock
- 40 g/1½ oz. vegan hard cheese, finely grated, plus extra to serve
- grated zest and freshly squeezed juice of 1 lemon
- 1 head of cauliflower (400 g/14 oz.), grated or blitzed in a food processor
- 100 g/2 cups baby kale leaves

SERVES 4

This risotto is made with half cauli 'rice' and half risotto rice. It has the creaminess of a traditional risotto, but the cauliflower gives it more nutritious value and is lower in carbohydrates.

Melt the oil in a large saucepan set over a low heat. Add the onion and cook for 10–15 minutes, until soft but not coloured.

Turn the heat up to medium, then pour in the risotto rice and stir for a few minutes, to ensure every grain is well coated in oil, then add the saffron and stir well. Pour in the white wine and let it bubble away for a couple of minutes, stirring regularly.

Begin ladling in the hot vegetable stock, bit by bit, stirring it through the rice and allowing each ladleful to become absorbed before adding the next. Continue slowly adding stock in this way for about 15–20 minutes until the rice is cooked through and the risotto is creamy.

Stir in the grated cheese, lemon zest and juice, grated cauliflower and baby kale and cook for a further 3 minutes. Serve with extra grated cheese on top.

MEXICAN RED RICE

- 200 g/7 oz. tomatoes
- 1 tablespoon vegetable oil
- ½ onion, finely chopped
- 1 garlic clove, sliced
- 1 red chilli/chile, chopped
- 200 g/1 cup long-grain rice, rinsed
- 250 ml/1 cup vegetable stock
- sea salt, to taste
- 50 g/½ cup frozen peas (optional)

SERVES 4

Tomatoes give a delicate sweetness to the rice here, with a touch of heat from the chilli/chile. Serve as a tasty side dish with roasted vegetables and a tomato salsa.

Begin by scalding the tomatoes. Pour boiling water over the ripe tomatoes in a heatproof bowl. Set aside for 1 minute, then drain and carefully peel off the skin using a sharp knife. Roughly chop, reserving any juices, and set aside.

Heat the oil in a heavy-bottomed saucepan or pot set over a medium heat. Add the onion and garlic and fry until softened. Add the chilli and fry for another minute, then add the chopped tomatoes with their juices. Increase the heat, stir well and cook until the tomatoes have broken down and form a thick paste.

Mix in the rice and pour over the stock. Season with salt, bring the mixture to the boil and add the frozen peas, if using. Cover, reduce the heat and cook for 10–15 minutes until the stock has been absorbed and the rice is cooked through.

Recipe photograph overleaf

TRAYBAKES

ROASTED CAULIFLOWER SALAD

- 1 head of cauliflower, cut into wedges
- 5 garlic cloves, crushed into a paste
- ½ bunch fresh thyme, leaves picked
- 3 tablespoons olive oil
- pinch of dried chilli flakes/ hot red pepper flakes
- 60 g/2¼ oz. capers, rinsed and drained
- 100 g/3½ oz. semi-dried tomatoes
- 200 g/7 oz. torn sourdough
- 20 g/1 cup (loosely packed) fresh parsley, leaves picked and roughly chopped
- 1 tablespoon balsamic reduction, to finish

SERVES 4

This simple roasted traybake salad is the perfect quick midweek meal and also works really well as a barbecue or cookout side dish.

Preheat the oven to 180°C fan/200°C/400°F/Gas 6.

Place the cauliflower in a large baking dish and rub with the crushed garlic, thyme and olive oil. Roast in the preheated oven for 30 minutes.

Remove from the oven and sprinkle with the dried chilli flakes, capers, semi-dried tomatoes and torn sourdough. Return to the oven for another 20 minute until the cauliflower is nicely browned.

Serve scattered with the chopped parsley and drizzled with the balsamic reduction.

VEGETABLE-LOADED NACHOS

- 250 g/2 cups butternut squash, cut into small 1.5 cm/½-inch cubes
- 1 tablespoon olive or avocado oil
- ½ teaspoon dried and ground chipotle or cayenne pepper
- tortilla chips
- 200 g/1 cup Barbecue Black Beans (see below), plus more as needed
- sea salt, to taste

TO SERVE

- 115 g/½ cup guacamole, plus more on the side
- 130 g/½ cup pico de gallo (or fresh salsa)
- 50 g/¼ cup Creamy Chipotle Dip (see below)
- 3 spring onions/scallions, thinly sliced

SERVES 4–6

The exact quantities for your nacho toppings will vary depending on the size of your nacho tray and your preference. The Barbecue Black Beans and Creamy Chipotle Dip make more than you'll need for these nachos, but luckily they are great in many other dishes like tacos and salads, too.

Preheat the oven to 180°C fan/200°C/400°F/Gas 6.

Spread the butternut squash cubes out on a baking sheet lined with baking parchment. Drizzle with the oil and sprinkle over the ground chipotle or cayenne pepper and salt to taste. Mix together so the squash is well coated in the seasoning. Roast in the preheated oven for about 25 minutes until golden and tender.

Turn the oven temperature down to 160°C fan/180°C/350°F/Gas 4.

Spread the tortilla chips out on the lined baking sheet – enough to fill the sheet generously in a thin layer. Scatter over the roasted butternut and then the barbecue black beans, spreading them out evenly across the baking sheet. Bake in the preheated oven for about 10 minutes.

Remove from the oven and top the nachos with small dollops of guacamole and pico de gallo or salsa, a drizzle of creamy chipotle dip and a scattering of spring onions.

Serve immediately either directly from the baking sheet or transfer the baking parchment onto a large plate.

BARBECUE BLACK BEANS

- avocado or olive oil, for frying
- 1 garlic clove, chopped
- 1 teaspoon smoked paprika
- ½ teaspoon ground cumin
- 400-g/14-oz. can black beans in their liquid
- 2 tablespoons tomato purée/paste
- 1 tablespoon pure maple syrup
- 60–120 ml/¼–½ cup vegetable stock
- sea salt, to taste

SERVES 4

Heat a little oil in a large pan with high sides over a medium-high heat. Add the garlic and spices and cook, stirring, for 1 minute. Add the beans with their liquid and stir to coat in the spices. Add the tomato purée and maple syrup, season with salt and stir. Turn the heat to medium-low, cover and simmer for 10 minutes. Add some stock if the mixture looks dry. Remove from heat and stand, covered, for 10 minutes before serving.

CREAMY CHIPOTLE DIP

- 75 g/⅓ cup tahini, mixed well
- 1 chipotle pepper in adobo sauce or ½ tablespoon chipotle paste
- 1 tablespoon adobo sauce from the pepper can (omit if using the paste)
- 1 tablespoon fresh lime juice
- 1 teaspoon pure maple syrup
- ½ teaspoon sea salt
- 1 garlic clove, peeled

MAKES ABOUT 235 ML/1 CUP

Place all the ingredients in a food processor and blend together with 75 ml/⅓ cup water until smooth. Add more water, if needed, to reach the desired consistency.

PORTABELLINI MUSHROOMS
WITH CANNELLINI BEANS & LEMON TAHINI DRESSING

- 500 g/1 lb. 2 oz. portabellini mushrooms, stalks removed
- 100 ml/⅓ cup plus 1 tablespoon extra virgin olive oil
- 2 garlic cloves, finely chopped
- 1 teaspoon fresh thyme leaves
- 4 generous handfuls of fresh baby spinach leaves
- 400-g/14-oz. can cannellini beans, drained and rinsed

LEMON TAHINI DRESSING
- 75 g/⅓ cup tahini paste
- zest and juice of 1 lemon
- 2 garlic cloves, grated

SERVES 3–4

Portabellini mushrooms have a really lovely, deliciously savoury flavour and are well worth seeking out, but at a pinch, you could use brown chestnut mushrooms as an alternative if you can't get hold of them.

Preheat the oven to 160°C fan/180°C/350°F/Gas 4.

Put the mushrooms on a baking sheet. Mix the oil, garlic and thyme together and spoon all but a tablespoon over the mushrooms. Bake for 10-15 minutes, until the mushrooms are cooked. Stir the spinach and beans together with the remaining spoonful of garlic and thyme oil, and spoon this around the cooked mushrooms.

Return everything to the oven for 4-5 minutes, until the spinach is lightly wilted and the beans are warm. Arrange everything on a serving platter and pour over any juices that are left in the pan.

Mix all the ingredients for the tahini dressing together in a bowl with 60-75 ml/¼-⅓ cup water and drizzle over the mushrooms before serving.

ROAST BUTTERNUT SQUASH
WITH LENTILS & POMEGRANATES

- 2 small butternut squash, halved and deseeded
- 4–5 tablespoons olive oil
- a handful of fresh thyme leaves
- 2 tablespoons freshly chopped rosemary
- 2 large leeks, trimmed and chopped
- 300 g/10½ oz. baby plum tomatoes
- 400-g/14-oz. can black beluga lentils
- sea salt and freshly ground black pepper

DRESSING
- 3½ tablespoons olive oil
- 3½ tablespoons pomegranate molasses

TO SERVE
- 50 g/scant ½ cup toasted pine nuts
- 3–4 tablespoons pomegranate seeds

SERVES 4

Roasting the squash in its skin gives the whole vegetable such a fabulous texture and the skin is unbelievably good to eat. This is good served with a rocket/arugula salad.

Preheat the oven to 170°C fan/190°C/375°F/Gas 5.

Lightly score a diamond pattern into the flesh of the squash using the tip of a sharp knife. Drizzle with a little of the oil, sprinkle with the thyme and rosemary, place on a flat baking sheet and bake for 15 minutes.

Remove the baking sheet from the oven and push the squash over to one side. Scatter the chopped leeks and tomatoes on the other side of the pan and drizzle with the remaining oil. Scatter with salt and freshly ground black pepper and return to the oven for another 20 minutes, until the flesh of the squash is soft and the leeks and tomatoes are lightly charred.

Scoop the leeks and tomatoes into a large bowl. Drain and rinse the lentils, and add them to the bowl.

Mix the olive oil and pomegranate molasses together for the dressing and add about half to the lentil mixture. Pile the mixture into the squash hollows and return the baking sheet to the oven. Bake for 5 minutes, until the lentil filling is just heated through.

Remove from the oven, drizzle over the remaining dressing, scatter with pine nuts and pomegranate seeds and add a good grinding of black pepper.

ROASTED HERITAGE BEETROOTS WITH BALSAMIC DRESSING

- 1 kg/2 lb. 3 oz. mixed heritage beetroots/beets, peeled and cut into wedges
- 3 red onions, cut into wedges
- 250 g/3½ cups chestnut mushrooms, sliced
- 135 ml/generous ½ cup olive oil
- 5–6 sprigs of freshly chopped rosemary
- 400-g/14-oz. can green lentils, drained and rinsed
- 3 tablespoons balsamic vinegar
- 1 teaspoon caster/granulated sugar
- 1 garlic clove, finely grated
- freshly chopped mixed herbs (dill, chives, parsley), to serve

SERVES 4

This is a pretty special traybake dish and is even more delicious when served with plenty of crusty bread for mopping up all of the lovely juices and flavours.

Preheat the oven to 170°C fan/190°C/375°F/Gas 5.

Arrange the beetroot over the base of a baking sheet. Add the onions and scatter the mushrooms evenly over the top. Drizzle with 3 tablespoons of the olive oil and scatter over the chopped rosemary. Roast for 45–50 minutes, until the beetroots are soft.

Spoon the lentils onto the baking sheet. Return to the oven for 5 minutes, until the lentils are heated through.

Mix the remaining olive oil, balsamic vinegar, sugar and garlic together.

Remove the baking sheet from the oven, drizzle over the dressing, scatter over the freshly chopped herbs and serve warm or at room temperature.

ROASTED WINTER VEGGIES & LENTILS

- 400 g/14 oz. parsnips, peeled and cut into batons
- 1 medium fennel bulb, cut into wedges
- 5–6 tablespoons olive oil
- 3 tablespoons brown rice syrup or maple syrup
- 1 medium cauliflower, broken into florets
- 2 small leeks, trimmed and sliced
- 1 small pointy cabbage, thickly sliced
- 1 teaspoon fennel seeds
- 400-g/14-oz. can green lentils, drained and rinsed
- sea salt and freshly ground black pepper
- dill or fennel fronds, to garnish

DRESSING
- 100 ml/generous ⅓ cup extra virgin olive oil
- 25 g/1 oz. grain mustard
- 2 tablespoons cider vinegar
- 15 g/½ oz. caster/granulated sugar
- zest of 1 lemon

SERVES 4

This one-pan medley really qualifies as roasted veggie heaven – the heat of the oven brings out the natural sweetness of each vegetable and creates the most delicious result.

Preheat the oven to 170°C fan/190°C/375°F/Gas 5.

Place the parsnip batons and fennel wedges in a large bowl and add half of the oil and the brown rice syrup or maple syrup. Toss to coat everything, and then arrange on a baking sheet. Roast for about 15 minutes, until the vegetables are beginning to soften.

Arrange the cauliflower florets over the baking sheet. Scatter the leeks evenly over the top. Cut the cabbage slices into halves or quarters, and lay them here and there over the baking sheet. Drizzle over the remaining oil, sprinkle with fennel seeds, and season. Return the baking sheet to the oven and roast for a further 20 minutes or so, until the vegetables are soft and slightly charred on the edges.

When the vegetables are cooked, spoon the lentils randomly but evenly over the vegetables and return the baking sheet to the oven for 5 minutes, until the lentils are just warmed through.

Meanwhile, whisk all the ingredients for the dressing together in a bowl. Remove the baking sheet from the oven, drizzle the dressing over the vegetables and garnish with dill or fennel fronds to serve.

CAULIFLOWER BRIAM

- 50 ml/3½ tablespoons extra virgin olive oil, plus extra if needed
- 200 g/7 oz. sweet potatoes, scrubbed and skins left on, sliced into rounds
- 12 cherry tomatoes
- 3 courgettes/zucchini, sliced into rounds
- 1 large aubergine/eggplant, sliced into rounds
- 1 large onion, sliced into rounds
- 3 garlic cloves, crushed
- 250 g/9 oz. sprouting cauliflower or normal cauliflower
- 300 g/10½ oz. passata/strained tomatoes
- 30 g/1 oz. fresh oregano, leaves picked
- sea salt and freshly ground black pepper

SERVES 6

A Greek-style vegetable bake that is delicious freshly made and warm, but even better the next day served at room temperature. This version includes sweet potatoes, which pair beautifully with the other flavours.

Preheat the oven to 200°C fan/220°C/425°F/Gas 7.

Place the olive oil, sweet potatoes, cherry tomatoes, courgettes, aubergine, onion, garlic, cauliflower and passata in a large ovenproof dish. Sprinkle with the oregano. Season generously with salt and pepper. Combine well with your hands and drizzle with extra oil, if needed.

Bake in the preheated oven for 30 minutes, then turn the oven temperature down to 180°C fan/200°C/400°F/Gas 6. Bake for another 20–30 minutes, or until the top has browned and the vegetables are tender; add a little water if the dish gets too dry. Leave to cool slightly before serving.

VEGETABLE & KIDNEY BEAN BAKE WITH AVOCADO HOLLANDAISE

- 1 onion, chopped
- 3 celery stalks, chopped
- 2 garlic cloves, finely chopped
- 3 sweet potatoes, peeled and diced
- 2 carrots, diced
- 2 yellow (bell) peppers, deseeded and cut into strips
- 1 red (bell) pepper, deseeded and cut into strips
- 250 g/9 oz. chestnut mushrooms, sliced
- 450 g/1 lb. cherry tomatoes
- 4–5 tablespoons olive oil
- 2 teaspoons ground cumin
- 2 teaspoons ground coriander
- 2 teaspoons chilli/chili powder
- 2 teaspoons caster/granulated sugar
- 600 ml/2½ cups passata/strained tomatoes
- 2 tablespoons good-quality tomato ketchup
- 400-g/14-oz. can red kidney beans, drained and rinsed
- 2 handfuls of fresh baby spinach leaves
- a handful of freshly chopped coriander/ cilantro
- sea salt and freshly ground black pepper

AVOCADO HOLLANDAISE
- 1 large, ripe avocado
- juice of ½ lemon
- 2 tablespoons olive oil

SERVES 4

This is a mild meat-free chilli/chili that doesn't pack too much of a punch, making it family-friendly, but chilli/chile-fiends could add some dried chilli/hot red pepper flakes, a slick of chilli oil or even a scattering of some freshly chopped chilli/chile. The avocado 'hollandaise' lifts the whole dish to another level, so do make sure to serve the two together.

Preheat the oven to 160°C fan/180°C/350°F/Gas 4.

Scatter the onion, celery and garlic into a deep roasting pan. Add the sweet potatoes, carrots, peppers, mushrooms and cherry tomatoes to the pan. Drizzle in the olive oil, add the spices and sugar, season with salt and freshly ground black pepper and roast for 20–35 minutes, until the vegetables have started to soften and brown.

Remove from the oven and stir in the passata and ketchup. Cook for a further 30 minutes. Remove from the oven, stir in the kidney beans, spinach and half of the coriander. Return to the oven for 5 minutes, until the spinach is just wilted. Scatter over the remaining coriander.

In the meantime, make the avocado hollandaise. Peel the avocado and remove the pit/stone. Chop the flesh and pop it into the bowl of a blender (alternatively, use a jug/pitcher and a stick blender). Add the lemon juice, olive oil and 3½ tablespoons water and whiz to a smooth purée. Season to taste, transfer to a small bowl and serve alongside the vegetable and kidney bean bake.

POTATO & ROSEMARY PIZZA

PIZZA BASE

- 500 g/3½–3⅔ cups strong plain bread flour
- 1 teaspoon fine sea salt
- 1 teaspoon caster/granulated sugar
- 7 g/¼ oz. sachet fast-action dried yeast
- 1 tablespoon olive oil
- about 300 ml/1¼ cups hand-hot water

TOPPING

- 600 g/1 lb. 5 oz. smallish floury potatoes, soaked and very thinly sliced (see introduction)
- 4 tablespoons olive oil
- 2 tablespoons finely chopped rosemary
- a large bunch of spring onions/scallions, chopped
- sea salt and freshly ground black pepper

SERVES 4

This vegan pizza is made from the kind of staples you generally have in the kitchen – and if you use fast-action yeast, it's doesn't take too long from start to finish either. If possible, cut and soak the potato slices in cold water for 30 minutes or so before making the pizza bases – this helps the potatoes crisp more efficiently.

Preheat the oven to 180°C fan/200°C/400°F/Gas 6.

Put the flour into a large bowl and stir in the salt and sugar. Add the yeast and mix well. Pour in the olive oil, and add enough hand-hot water to bring the mixture together into a soft, but not sticky dough. Knead the dough for 5–10 minutes until smooth. Divide the dough into two and roll each piece into a rectangle to fit the base of two baking sheets.

Drain the water from the potatoes and rinse them under running cold water one final time. Dry thoroughly on paper towels or a clean kitchen towel. Toss them into a large bowl with the olive oil, rosemary and a generous sprinkling of salt flakes and black pepper, until all the slices are evenly coated.

Scatter the spring onions between the two bases. Top with the potato slices, overlapping the potato edges very slightly, until the bases are covered. Bake the pizzas for about 20 minutes or so, until the potatoes are cooked and crispy golden at the edges. Cut into squares and serve at once.

CORN & TOFU PIE

- 500 g/1 lb. 2 oz./17 sheets of filo/phyllo pastry
- 100 g/½ cup olive oil

FILLING
- 250 g/2 cups sweetcorn/corn kernels (fresh, canned, or frozen and thawed)
- 500 g/1 lb. 2 oz. medium-soft tofu
- 2 tablespoons olive oil
- 2¼ teaspoons sea salt
- 460 ml/2 cups soya/soy milk
- 230 ml/1 cup hot water
- 130 g/1 cup fine polenta/cornmeal

SERVES 6–8

A vegan version of Greek filo/phyllo pie, this dish makes an excellent lunch or dinner and is very filling. Corn kernels add a nice sweetness and texture to the smooth tofu layers, but using some blanched greens instead of corn is also a delicious variation worth trying. Serve with a big bowl of salad, or a cup of non-dairy yogurt if you're in a hurry.

First make the filling. If using canned sweetcorn/corn, wash it and drain well. In a big bowl, crumble the tofu with your fingers and add the sweetcorn, oil, salt, milk and hot water and mix until well combined. Whisk in the polenta. The filling should be moderately smooth besides the sweetcorn and small pieces of tofu.

Preheat the oven to 160°C fan/180°C/350°F/Gas 4. Oil a 20 x 30-cm/8 x 12-inch baking pan.

If the sheets of filo are bigger than your baking pan, cut them to size. Don't worry if a sheet tears as you can easily patch up any damage – only the top 2 sheets need to stay undamaged.

Place a sheet of filo in the baking pan. (Cover the remaining sheets with clingfilm/plastic wrap to prevent them from drying out.) Brush oil lightly over the sheet. Cover with another sheet and oil it. Repeat this process with 2 more sheets.

Spread one-fifth of the filling evenly over the top with a spatula.

Cover with one sheet, oil lightly and cover with a second sheet (this one doesn't need oiling). Spread one-fifth of the filling evenly over the top. Continue like this until you have used up all the filling, and you have 5 layers each of filling and filo sheets.

To finish, brush a little oil over the remaining 5 sheets of filo and lay them on top of the pie – the 2 best, undamaged sheets should be on the top. Tuck in any pastry or filling sticking out of the pan by pushing a spatula between the pie and the sides of the pan. Use a sharp knife to score 16 squares into the pastry.

Bake in the preheated oven for 45 minutes, or until the top turns golden brown and the pie isn't wobbly or soft to the touch.

Allow to cool completely (at least 5 hours, or overnight) in the pan before serving.

ROASTED MEDITERRANEAN VEGETABLES
WITH BALSAMIC DRESSING

- 2 red onions, cut into wedges
- 1 large courgette/zucchini, sliced
- 1 medium aubergine/eggplant, cut into bite-sized chunks
- 1 red (bell) pepper, deseeded and cut into strips
- 1 yellow (bell) pepper, deseeded and cut into strips
- 1 orange (bell) pepper, deseeded and cut into strips
- 400 g/14 oz. cherry tomatoes
- 5 tablespoons olive oil
- a good scattering of fresh thyme leaves
- 3 tablespoons balsamic vinegar
- sea salt and freshly ground black pepper
- fresh basil leaves, to garnish

SERVES 4

When the ingredients call for '1 large courgette/zucchini', this doesn't mean the sort that is on the verge of classification as a small marrow – huge courgettes/zucchinis might look fairly impressive on the outside, but the flesh can become quite lacking in flavour, as the water content rises and the seeds become bigger – often giving the vegetable a slightly bitter taste. Make sure to roast until the vegetables are looking a little charred at the edges here and there – it will take the best part of an hour, but will reward with bags of flavour.

Preheat the oven to 170°C fan/190°C/375°F/Gas 5.

Scatter the onion wedges, courgette, aubergine and peppers over a baking sheet. Leave the tomatoes whole and scatter the tomatoes over. Drizzle everything with the oil, season with salt, freshly ground black pepper and lots of fresh thyme leaves. Cook for about 50–60 minutes, turning everything halfway through the cooking time, until the vegetables are shiny and soft and lightly charred at the edges.

Drizzle over the balsamic vinegar, garnish with fresh basil leaves and serve warm or at room temperature.

CARAMELIZED FENNEL & HERITAGE CARROTS WITH CITRUS DRESSING

- 2 fennel bulbs
- 600 g/1 lb. 5 oz. heritage carrots
- 4–5 tablespoons olive oil
- freshly squeezed juice of 1 lemon
- 2 teaspoons caster/granulated sugar
- 4 juicy oranges
- a large handful of chopped mixed herbs (parsley, coriander/cilantro, dill, chives, etc.)
- sea salt and freshly ground black pepper

DRESSING
- 100 ml/generous ⅓ cup olive oil
- zest and juice of 1 lemon
- 1 teaspoon caster/granulated sugar

SERVES 4

Warm, caramelized fennel and colourful heritage carrots make magnificent bedfellows to thin slices of fresh juicy oranges. Don't skimp on the herbs.

Preheat the oven to 170°C fan/190°C/375°F/Gas 5.

Trim the fennel bulbs, then cut them in half, from root to tip. Cut each half into three or four wedges. Arrange over a baking sheet. Cut the carrots in half or into quarters along their length, depending on the size of the carrots. Arrange them over the sheet with the fennel wedges. Drizzle over the oil and lemon juice and scatter over the sugar. Roast for about 25–30 minutes, until the vegetables are soft and slightly charred at the edges.

In the meantime, top, tail and peel the oranges and cut into thin slices. Mix the oil, lemon juice and sugar together for the dressing, and squeeze in any juice from the end pieces of orange peel. Season with a little salt and black pepper.

Remove the pan from the oven and transfer everything to a platter. Drizzle over the citrus dressing, scatter with the fresh herbs and serve.

SWEET POTATO, SAFFRON & AUBERGINE CHORBA

- 2 onions, chopped
- 2 sweet potatoes (about 400 g/ 14 oz.), peeled and cut into bite-sized chunks
- 1 aubergine/eggplant, diced
- 100 g/3½ oz. cherry tomatoes, sliced
- 4 tablespoons olive oil
- 2 tablespoons ras el hanout spice mix
- 1 litre/quart vegetable stock
- a generous pinch of saffron threads
- 100 g/generous ½ cup quick-cook spelt or basmati rice
- 400-g/14-oz. can chickpeas/ garbanzo beans
- a handful of freshly chopped coriander/cilantro

SERVES 4

Chorba is a hearty soup or stew and is popular in many North African countries. Serve it with some thick vegan yogurt, a slick of chilli/chile oil and some good crusty bread.

Preheat the oven to 170°C fan/190°C/375°F/Gas 5.

Add the onions and the sweet potatoes to a large high-sided baking dish. Add the aubergine and cherry tomatoes. Drizzle the oil over the vegetables and stir in the ras el hanout spice, so that everything is well coated. Transfer the dish to the oven and roast for about 20–25 minutes, until the vegetables have taken on a golden colour.

Pour the stock into the dish and add the saffron and the spelt (or rice). Drain and rinse the chickpeas, add to the dish, and give everything a good stir round. Return the dish to the oven and cook for a further 25–30 minutes, until the spelt (or rice) is soft and the soup has thickened. Scatter with freshly chopped coriander and serve.

CRUNCHY POTATO STRUDEL

- 6 filo/phyllo dough sheets (35 x 30 cm/13¾ x 12 inch)
- 90 g/scant ½ cup sunflower oil, plus extra for oiling
- 4 large potatoes, peeled
- 180 g/1½ cups onions, diced
- ¼ teaspoon sea salt
- ¼–½ teaspoon crushed black pepper
- 100 ml/scant ½ cup hot vegetable stock

MAKES 12 PIECES

Everybody loves potatoes and everybody loves crunchy filo/phyllo pastry, so this is a safe recipe for picky eaters and vegan-sceptical guests as it's a real crowd pleaser!

Take the filo sheets out of the fridge 30 minutes before making the strudel to prevent the leaves from cracking during baking.

Place one sheet of filo on a dry work surface, with the longer side facing you (keep the remaining filo sheets covered with clingfilm/plastic wrap to prevent them from drying out). In a small bowl, mix 3 tablespoons water with 4 tablespoons of the oil. With a silicone spatula, brush the filo sheet lightly with the oil and water mixture. Top it with another sheet of filo sheet (the second one doesn't need oiling).

Dice 2 potatoes, and grate the other two. In a large bowl, mix the potatoes with the onions, salt and pepper.

Preheat the oven to 160°C fan/180°C/350°F/Gas 4. Oil a 23 x 30-cm/ 9 x 12-inch baking pan.

Spread one-third portion of the potato filling on the bottom edge of the 2 filo sheets in a 6-cm/2½-inch wide strip, leaving a 2-cm/¾-inch edge on the sides to prevent the filling from falling out. Roll carefully into a nice strudel and place it in the pre-oiled baking pan. Repeat with the remaining sheets and filling to make 3 strudels. Brush them with oil and use a sharp knife to cut partially through the dough, marking 4 slices per strudel. Splash 2 tablespoons of the hot vegetable stock over each strudel.

Bake in the oven for 10 minutes. Pour over some hot vegetable stock again and repeat until you have no liquid left. This strudel will need another 25–30 minutes to turn brown and crispy on the top and edges, but soft and juicy in the middle. Serve warm or cold, with a crisp green salad.

BERBERE ROASTED CAULIFLOWER WITH APRICOTS & MUHAMMARA

MUHAMMARA
- 2 red (bell) peppers, deseeded and cut into strips
- 3 tablespoons olive oil
- 1 teaspoon ground cumin
- 50 g/½ cup walnut pieces
- 1 garlic clove, finely chopped
- 30 g/½ cup fresh breadcrumbs
- 1 tablespoon pomegranate molasses
- 1 tablespoon good-quality tomato ketchup
- 1 teaspoon dried chilli/hot red pepper flakes
- sea salt and freshly ground black pepper

CAULIFLOWER
- 1 good-sized cauliflower
- 3-4 tablespoons olive oil
- 1½ tablespoons berbere spice mix (see page 99)
- 50 g/scant ½ cup toasted pine nuts
- 200 g/1⅓ cups dried apricots, halved

TO SERVE
- 2 tablespoons pomegranate molasses
- 3 tablespoons olive oil
- a handful of freshly chopped coriander/cilantro
- a small handful of freshly chopped parsley
- mint leaves, to garnish

SERVES 4

Berbere is a punchy hot spice mix from Ethiopia – making your own means you can adjust the heat to suit. Muhammara is a glorious, dip-into or dollop-on invention that hails from Syria, but is now popular all across the whole Levantine area.

Preheat the oven to 170°C fan/190°C/375°F/Gas 5.

To make the muhammara, toss the red peppers with 2 tablespoons of the oil and the cumin and arrange the strips over a large baking sheet. Roast for 20 minutes, until softened and slightly charred.

Transfer to a blender and whiz to a purée. Add the walnuts, garlic, breadcrumbs, pomegranate molasses, ketchup, chilli and remaining oil and whiz again, until you have a lightly textured purée with the consistency of whipped cream. If the mixture is a little too thick, add some warm water. Season and set aside.

For the cauliflower, break the cauliflower into small florets and toss in a bowl with the olive oil and Berbere spice mix. Spread over the baking sheet used for the peppers and roast for about 15 minutes, until the cauliflower is cooked, but still has a little bite. Scatter over the pine nuts and apricots and return to the oven for a few minutes to warm through.

Stir the pomegranate molasses and oil together and spoon over the cauliflower. Scatter with the freshly chopped herbs and mint leaves and serve with the muhammara.

INDEX

CREDITS

RECIPE CREDITS

GHILLIE BASAN
Aubergine Tagine
Baby Courgette Stew
Preserved Lemons
Roasted Potato & Fennel
  Tagine

LIZ FRANKLIN
Baked Oat Milk Porridge
Bay-scented Coconut Milk
  Black Rice
Berbere Roasted Cauliflower
  with Apricots
Caramelized Fennel &
  Heritage Carrots
Cinnamon Spiced Bruschetta
Easy Baked Lentils & Root
  Veg
Portabellini Mushrooms with
  Cannellini Beans & Lemon
  Tahini Dressing
Potato & Rosemary Pizza
Roast Butternut Squash with
  Black Beluga Lentils
Roast Rhubarb, Blackberry
  & Blueberry Compote
Roasted Heritage Beetroots
  with Rosemary Crisps &
  Balsamic Dressing
Roasted Mexican Vegetables
  with Balsamic Dressing
Roasted Traybake Veggies
  & Lentils
Slow-baked Pecan & Cocoa
  Nib Granola
Sweet Potato, Saffron &
  Aubergine Chorba
Vegetable & Kidney Bean
  Bake

TONIA GEORGE
Lentil, Spinach & Cumin Broth

DUNJA GULIN
Adzuki Beans with Amaranth
Corn & Tofu Pie

Crunchy Potato Strudel
Healing Miso Broth
One-pot Miso Noodle Soup
Tofu Scramble

KATHY KORDALIS
Caribbean Sweet Potato
  & Coconut Soup
Cauliflower Briam
Cauliflower, Butternut
  Squash & Chickpeas
Cauliflower Larb
Cauliflower Risotto
Cauliflower, Vegetable
  & Bean Ragu
Cream of Cauliflower Soup
Dan Dan Cauliflower Soup
Grainy Porridge Three Ways
Laksa with Cauliflower
Roasted Cauliflower Salad
Thai Green Cauli Curry

JENNY LINFORD
Harissa Potato & Lentil Salad
Mexican Red Rice
Miso Potato Soup
Mushroom & Bean Chilli
Mushroom, Spinach &
  Coconut Curry
One-pot Chickpea, Chard
  & Potato
Persian-style Saffron Rice
Tarka Tomato Dal
Tomato Curry

HANNAH MILES
Massaman Potato Soup
Spinach & Nutmeg Soup
Sunshine Soup
Sweet Potato, Coriander
  & Maple Soup
Three Bean Soup

LOUISE PICKFORD
Artichoke & Broad Bean
  Paella
Baked Rice with Chickpeas
  & Raisins

Bean & Pea Paella
Vegetable Paella

LEAH VANDERVELDT
Barbecue Black Beans
Basic Avocado Dip
Chickpea 'Tikka' Masala
Chocolate & Coconut
  Granola
Classic Mixed Oatmeal
  Porridge
Creamy Chipotle Dip
Creamy Sweet Potato
  & White Beans
Garlic Yogurt Dip
Green Kitchari Bowl
Green Thai Soup
Mexican Butternut Squash
  & Black Bean
Moroccan-spiced Lentils
Pumpkin Coconut Soup
Red Lentil Dahl
Spring Vegetable Soup
Vegetable Loaded Nachos

**LAURA WASHBURN
HUTTON**
Greek Summer Vegetable
  Stew

PHOTOGRAPHY CREDITS

ED ANDERSON
Page 11.

TIM ATKINS
Page 137.

JAN BALDWIN
Pages 149, 160.

MARTIN BRIGDALE
Page 82.

PETER CASSIDY
Pages 69, 124.

MOWIE KAY
Pages 25, 56, 58, 62, 70, 90,
  102, 108, 121, 123, 128,
  140.

ALEX LUCK
Pages 42, 45, 46, 49, 53, 54,
  59.

DAVID MUNNS
Page 92.

STEVE PAINTER
Pages 1, 14, 17, 18, 19, 20,
  22, 23, 36, 51, 57, 63, 64,
  71, 77, 78, 81, 98, 106, 117,
  132, 135, 136, 139, 143,
  144, 148, 151, 152, 156.

WILLIAM REAVELL
Pages 27, 101, 155.

NASSIMA ROTHACKER
Pages 103, 125.

CHRISTOPHER SCHOLEY
Page 104.

TOBY SCOTT
Pages 38, 41.

YUKI SUGIURA
Page 37.

IAN WALLACE
Pages 2-3, 27, 28, 35, 47, 83,
  91, 109, 112, 115, 119, 120,
  133, 163.

KATE WHITAKER
Pages 4, 43, 74, 84, 129.

CLARE WINFIELD
Pages 5, 7, 8, 10, 13, 15, 16,
  30, 31, 33, 34, 50, 52, 60,
  65, 66, 67, 72, 73, 75, 86,
  89, 93, 94, 97, 111, 116, 118,
  126, 131, 141, 149, 167.